Out of the Dark
Swadlincote Stories

Monica Hudson
Joan Jones
Roland Toon
Eileen Harvey
Christine Liversuch

With

Gill Johnson
Ian Daley

South Derbyshire Literature Development 1998

Published by South Derbyshire Literature Development, Civic Offices, Civic Way, Swadlincote, Derbyshire DE11 0AH.

Photos:
Tony and Trissie Gardner (pages 15,17,19,23,27,37,54,58,63,84,93,97,103,119,127,133,165) Evelyn Harrison (pages 66,69), Stuart Haywood (page 162) Monica Hudson (page 75), Joan Jones (pages 49,61,81, back cover) Jim Mansfield (page 155) Keith Mason (pages 107,116) Graham Nutt (page 46, 146, 179) Cliff Salisbury (pages 40,43) Marlene and Warwick Sibson (pages 150, 158, 175) John Smith (page 123) Peter Thornton (pages 29,45,113,130) From 'Swad Words, Swad Pictures', Chris Beech (pages 6,8,10,33,50,71,87,90,137,140, front cover)

Cover Design: Paul Miller of Ergo Design
ISBN: 1 899661 25 5
Printed FM Repro, Liversedge

The book has been funded by South Derbyshire District Council and East Midlands Arts

The results of two complementary projects involving the South Derbyshire Writers' Group can be seen in this book. The first, 'Swad Words, Swad Pictures' was a project funded by South Derbyshire's Council for Voluntary Services, South Derbyshire District Council's Arts Development Grant and the Coalfields Rural Initiative Fund 1998/9. This involved professional photographer, Chris Beech working with the group to devise a series of photographs based upon the group's writings. Many of Chris' photographs are collected here within the book, with the whole collection forming a touring exhibition of the area later this year.

The second project, 'Sounds Like Swad', was made possible through a successful application to the National Lottery's 'Arts For Everyone Express Scheme'. This allowed for the group to learn radio writing and production skills in the development of an hour long audio programme. Writer and broadcaster Graham Sellors worked with the group on the project which blends local speech with a scripted narration, much of the latter appearing within this book. Graham's words are marked in this book by a radio symbol. A cassette of the project will be available shortly.

For further information on Literature and Community Publishing in the area contact:
Literature Development, Derbyshire County Council, Libraries and Heritage Department, County Hall, Matlock, DE4 3AG Tel: 01629 580000
The South Derbyshire Writer's Group would welcome your stories and like to discuss any material you feel may be of interest to local readers, contact treasurer, Monica Hudson at:
6, Church Cottages, Swadlincote, Derbyshire, DE11 8LE
People Express are the Community Arts organisation for the area and will provide help and advice on projects in many art forms including literature and photography. Contact:
People Express Arts, Gresley Old Hall, Gresley Wood Road, Swadlincote, DE11 9QW Tel: 01283 552962

The South Derbyshire Writers' Group would like to thank the following:

East Midlands Arts and all members of South Derbyshire District Council's Leisure Services Committee. Special thanks to Councillor Mike Lauro, whose advocacy of literature and the arts have been a constant encouragement throughout the project, and to the two key people responsible for supporting the book - South Derbyshire District Council's Recreation Services Officer, Chris Mason and East Midlands Arts Literature Officer, Sue Stewart.

Other members of the District Council's staff deserving thanks are the Recreation and Administration division especially those who have undertaken much of the initial work upon the manuscript including; Sally Cope, Pam Wilson, Sue Sayers, Jane Palfreyman, Rita McGoldrick, John Porter and Steve Sheppard.

We have been fortunate in enlisting the support of countless individuals and organisations who have supported both the group and the project. We thank in particular, Christine Smith-Holmes, Tony and Trissie Gardner, Graham Nutt, Graham Hunt, Donna Salmond, Stuart and Rhona Haywood and Peter Thornton. We also thank Derbyshire County Council's Director of Libraries and Heritage, Martin Molloy, Deputy Director, Jaci Brumwell, and District Librarian Polly Jemison, who together with the staff of Swadlincote Library have helped us in so many ways with the book's progress. We have also received huge support and advice from Julie Holdway and Esther Davis at South Derbyshire's Arts Organisation, *People Express.* Thanks to Brian Vertigen, Killoran Wills, Andy Parker and Bill Pritchard at the *Burton Mail* and to South Derbyshire District Council's Press Officer, Sue Grief who did so much to bring the *Seams Like Swad* column to fruition. Thanks also to Jan Rodgers, Ashley Franklin and Mike Bettison at BBC Radio Derby whose support and promotion of the project and its audio counterpart, *Sounds Like Swad* have been immensely helpful to us.

We also thank the following professional workers in the field of community literature development from whom we've learnt so much about story collection and book production: to storyteller, Roy Dyson, for his skill in training us on the recording equipment and preparing interviewees; to storyteller, Mike Dunstan, for all his residency work in creative transcriptions which can be seen in some of the 'spoken poems' that appear in the book; to Graham Sellors, whose workshops on autobiographical writing and his radio residency work have added another perspective to our writing; to Gill Johnson, our Literature Development Officer for her dedication to and enthusiasm for our work and finally to Ian Daley at Yorkshire Art Circus, whose patience, sensitivity and skill in handling and helping us to shape the material into an edited book has been invaluable.

Thanks to those individuals who have loaned us their precious photos from private collections and to everyone who has helped us through contacts, letters and phone calls, a big thank-you. We are very grateful for all your help and information.

Peter Thornton
Arnold Webster
Evelyn Harrison
Colin Neale
Claire Edmonds
Ron Edmonds
G.H. Taylor
Liz Unwin
Stuart Haywood
Rhona Haywood
Rita McGoldrick
Polly Jemison
Vera Archer
Margaret Fessey
Pat Cowlishaw
Jenny Burley
Graham Nutt
Mr. Baker
Mary Poulson
Nita White
Arthur Timms
Wilfred Clamp
Jim Smith
Reg Large
Rose Large
Tim Chambers
John Budworth
Eric Sharrod
John Wilson
Christine Liversuch
Paul Liversuch
John Bailey
Eric Johnstone
Ernest Sutton
Norman Venning
Philip Osborne
Kenneth Roy Taylor

Mary Hyman
George 'Snowy' Smith
Paul Glover
Ann Marshall
Reg Reed
Betty Orme
Freda Budworth
Lillian Marriot
Deborah Rutter
Gordon Sharpe
Ted Pates
Tony Gardner
Trissie Gardner
Don Thompson
Judith Price Davis
Bob Jones
Joan Jones
Nora Wilkins
Kath Gardner
Iris Johnson
Derek Kinsey
Terry Jones
Christine Smith-Holmes
Cllr Ford
Jim Mansfied
Marlene Sibson
Warwick Sibson
Cyril Clamp
Derek Stephenson
Phyllis Wright
Monica Hudson
Roland Toon
Eileen Harvey
Norma Johnstone
Eileen Sabin Taylor

Mary Buckley
Lillian Illsley
Ken Illsley
Walter Perry
Jack Harding
Vera Morton
Vera Hextall
Phyllis Eyre
Francis May Draycott
Amelia Ann Woodward
Cyril Smith
Ken Spencer
Winnie Spencer
Mabel Jackson
Clara Davis
Joan Whetton
Beryl Greening
Nevel Stanier
Mr E. Wilson
Mr B. Woodward
Mr Cyril Thompson
Arthur Fairweather
K. Trussell
T. Harrison
C. Smith
D. Bird
B. Collier
L. Ayre
W. Barratt
L. Stone
R. Sharpe
W. Eley
C. Wardle
J. Hogg
G. Mould
R. Redfern

G. Pickering
C. Wileman
Brian Gunner
Eddie Wadsworth
F.J. Bloor
Mrs M. Bath
Sam Webster
Jennifer Hunt
Mr Green
Cliff Salisbury
Ernest Smith
Kevin Mason
Peter Birch
Frances Fairbrother
Patrick Smith
Mr Moon
Mrs Alexander
Janet Mansfield
Kathleen Edwards
Bill Shorthose
Mrs M. Miller
Chris Coleman
Gerrald Parker
Mary Shaw
May Crofts
Ruth Matthews
Morris Colborne
Mr Staley
Mrs Ward
Arthur 'Pud' Rice
Frances May Draycott
Gladys Adams
Mr Steve Boardman-Wood
Patty Whetton
Mr Dowell
Mr Barry Baker

A visitor to South Derbyshire in 1998 would see little physical evidence of coal mining, clay pipe works and potteries; the industries upon which the livelihoods of so many of its people used to depend. Even the terrible scarring and devastation of their landscape has all but healed.

Thankfully the heritage of that era has not yet completely disappeared and while ever the memories remain and the stories are handed from generation to generation, we shall know of those times and perhaps wonder at the courage, fortitude and stoicism of our forebears.

Some three to four years ago, the District Council and East Midlands Arts established a Literature Development initiative in South Derbyshire. Our Literature Development Officer, Gill Johnson has encouraged a number of writing projects in which many local people have been involved and in which they have discovered their literary potential.

The Council is pleased and proud to have encouraged in spirit and with finance this latest and most ambitious project of the South Derbyshire Writers' Group, a record of the area's history entitled, *Out of the Dark*.

Please don't let that word *history* make you put down this book, for this is no dry tome of dates and facts. This is the history of a time and a place told in the words of the people who were there. It is a treasure chest of great stories, sad stories, funny and incredible stories. They were gathered together by the Writers' Group and as well as the written stories, there is an archive on audio tape, much of which is in the unique dialect of the area. The whole project represents many months of painstaking research and the result is a book which perfectly brings together art and heritage. I hope it is the first of many.

The great humour, energy and generosity of spirit of South Derbyshire people is all here in these pages; the qualities that have brought the district, 'Out of the dark' and looking to the new millenium in a spirit of confidence and optimism, as the fastest growing district in Derbyshire and indeed one of the fastest in the country.

Councillor Mike Lauro
Chair of South Derbyshire District Council's
Leisure Services Committee

In 1996, a special project began in South Derbyshire to bring alive the stories of the mining years and to bring about a book worthy of those people who had shaped our past.

A number of local writers got together and formed the South Derbyshire Writers' Group and they transcribed, contributed and edited those recorded stories which not only featured the miners and their lives, but stories from the pit and pot workers, highlighting the people and town of Swadlincote itself.

It's been a difficult job to pull all of the written and spoken stories together in one volume but we hope you'll agree that the stories we've collected, go some way to reflect our rich cultural and social heritage.

Once we got going with our research, writing and recording, and spurred on by the success of our column, *Seams Like Swad* in the *Burton Mail*, we found similar stories and memories cropping up again and again. Remembering the success of another book about the area published a few years ago by People Express, *Stitches in Time,* the putting together of this book has been a bit like stitching a tapestry together. We used the threads of stories given to us from local people and slowly, a picture began to emerge - a kaleidoscope of characters and incidents from the past - emerging larger than life to live once again within these pages.

We've collected so much material over the past two years that it's been sadly impossible to include every single contribution - we would have needed a few more thousand pages for that! We hope though that we've compiled a representative and memorable selection of those subjects dearest to those of us in the area and we hope you'll agree that such stories do justice to Swad peoples' friendliness, loyalty, bravery and undeniable sense of fun.

One of the important points to make about the book is that it doesn't claim to be a complete, accurate or authoritative overview of the area. It's more of a selection of those stories and memories that people chose to share with us, telling us their tales in their own inimitable way, each story shaped by their own unique memory and experience. After all, the thing that makes Swadlincote the place it is, are the people themselves, and we've tried to let their voices come through.

We hope that the stories you'll read in here, trigger off a wealth of memories in your own mind and that you may choose to share some of them with us in the future. We certainly see this book as a beginning - a starting point to bring other stories and indeed other books 'out of the dark.'

The South Derbyshire Writers' Group

chapter one
Growing Up

Where it all starts

Cupped in the hills' rough hands
Hewn and moulded out of coal and clay
Ringed with pits, till they took them away
On a limb in South Derbyshire, Swadlincote stands.

The ambulance pulled away from the kerb and with it went the last of my childhood. Twelve years old and my mother has left me to do her job. It's not fair! I'm not ready yet! Yes, I want a house to look after and children to care for. But *not* this house and *not* my four sisters! In my world of tears, anger and self pity it took me some time to realise that our next door neighbour had her arm across my shoulder giving it a shake and was talking to me. At my blank look she repeated what she had said, "Come on, my girl, we've got work to do, and you can tell me all about it." Head bent, I sullenly sniffed and scuffed my way down the path to our back door, which led directly into the kitchen. Mrs. Clamp followed me in, picked up the kettle from the electric stove and went to fill it at the sink, while I stood in the middle of the small square room, stoically ignoring her.

"Right, kettle on first. Then while it boils we'll strip your Mam's bed and put them bloody sheets in soak while we have a cuppa." She had all my attention now. Mrs. Clamp never swore, not like old Mrs. Smith the other side who was always swearing at her Tony. Besides, Mrs. Clamp went to Chapel. "Come on, girl, stop catching flies. We have to get these sheets ready to go back on the bed for when your Mam comes out of 'ospital." I closed my mouth and mumbled "She won't come back. Nobody comes out of hospital when they go in by ambulance."

"Dunna talk so daft, lass, my Tommy's bin took twice from pit in an ambulance and 'e's all right in't 'e. Now let's get this job done, I've got things of me own to do you know." With that she bustled through to the living room, poked at the fire and made it up. While I trudged upstairs on legs like lead to strip the bed that I was sure my Mam would never need again.

By the time I went back down stairs with my arms full of bloodied sheets, there were two cups of steaming tea on the draining board and Mrs. Clamp was in the bathroom, next to the kitchen. She had half filled the bath with cold water and was filling the copper with hot, which was heated from the fire in the living room. She had already transferred some of that fire to start a blaze in the fire box under the copper.

"OK, my girl, put them sheets in soak, and mind you poke 'em down well. Then we'll have a drink while the water comes up."

Following her into the living room, both hands round my cup, trying to steal some warmth for my icy fingers, I found her sitting, elbows on the table, sipping at her drink. The table stood under the window and I sat with my tea untouched staring out, not seeing a thing. After some time Mrs. Clamp said, "Now, lass, drink up and tell me what happened."

I took a long gulp of my tea, then poured out all the events of the morning. How an hour after my Dad had gone to work our Mam had called me and said to get the three girls up and ready for school. How I was to stay at home today and help here with the baby, as Mam had been up all night with pains and she needed some sleep. How, when the girls had gone off to school, Mam had told me to go and phone the doctor and tell him that she was bleeding quite badly. How the doctor had said he would come straight away. Finally, with a voice cracking with tears, I screeched, "But he didn't come to make Mam better, he brought an ambulance to take her away to die."

Mrs. Clamp let me cry myself out. Then in her usual quiet manner said, "Well now child, let's get this straight shall we? First of all, when your Mam went to have your baby sister last month, she went into hospital and come out again, didn't she?" she waited. Looking up with watery, defiant eyes, I whispered a doubtful "Yes." "Well, when she had the baby her inside got shook up some and didn't go together again right. So now the doctor has to have her back again to put it right. Right?" I did so want to believe her. After all, Mrs. Clamp never told fibs, she went to Chapel didn't she? "I suppose." This answer came with a little more voice and a little less doubt. Suddenly remembering what I was at home from school for, I jumped up and cried, "Oh, where is the baby?" "Calm down lass, while you were upstairs, I took her next door to Granny Smith, she'll be all right there till we get this place sorted."

We did the washing together. After wringing out the sheets from the bath, we put them in the new electric washing machine. Mrs. Clamp had another pot of tea whilst I vacuumed and dusted Mam's room. "Mam was sure to be pleased when she came back, to a tidy room and clean sheets." Mrs. Clamp had said. But I still had my doubts.

By the time I had finished doing the rest of the house, Mrs. Clamp had boiled the sheets and cleared up the kitchen and bathroom. Her son John had put out the clothes line so Mrs. Clamp could show me how to hang out the sheets without dragging them in the dirt of the garden path. Mouth full of pegs, as instructed I threw one end of the sheet over my shoulder then reached up for the line. When one of the edges was safely pegged on I struggled to find the other, which had, by now, been wrapped round my neck by the wind. I finally managed to secure the other end to the line and stood watching with pride as the sheet billowed out like the sail of a ship. The next one was easier and the pillow cases were simple.

As we walked back up the garden Granny Smith came out of her kitchen door. Over one arm and perched on her hip was my sister, pink faced and drooling. In her other hand was a dinner plate piled high with sandwiches. "Come on, you two, this should keep us going till we do the dinner for the men folk."

I brewed a fresh pot of tea and we sat at the table eating the potted meat sandwiches while the two ladies gave me instruction on everything from how best to clean the outside lavatory, to the best way of cooking the cheaper cuts of meat. I didn't argue with them, or tell them that my Mam had already taught me most of what they were telling me. Or that I would do things the way I wanted to, but I munched more than my share of the sandwiches while they talked.

When we had finished our meal and washed up it was time to feed the baby. I was shown how to make the feed, cool it to the right temperature then settled into a chair, watched over by both the ladies, I started to feed my little sister. Mrs. Clamp and Granny Smith drank more tea and haggled over the best ways of looking after the child. Whilst I fed her, winded her, changed her nappy and had her fast asleep in the big pram before they finished off the pot.

The meal we had that day, when my Dad and the three girls came home, was provided by the neighbours. Mrs. Clamp made cottage pie and Granny Smith one of her special apple pies. Our Dad said it was better than Mam's but we girls told Mam in the notes we wrote to her that we liked hers much better. Dad took the notes and some flowers from Mr. Twiggs' allotment with him that night when he went to our Mam. He went in the van borrowed from the shop and everybody round us watched as he drove off down the street.

The days soon fell into a routine. Dad had written a note to my school asking if I could miss assembly and leave at half past three instead of four o'clock. I could then get my sisters off to Junior School, make sure the baby was delivered to a neighbour and be home in time to get the tea. I loved any sort of sports so I really enjoyed running to and from school. I often timed myself if John, from next door, would loan me his watch for the day.

My mother came home from hospital two weeks from that terrible Friday and the neighbours were in and out of our house all day. Not one person came without bringing a small gift for my Mam. There were flowers and cakes and pies and even a packet of butter. But things were never quite the same for me. I had taken on responsibilities and enjoyed being needed. I'm sure that fortnight was the start of what has been my role in life, to 'mother' anyone and everyone who I come into contact with. I can only hope I have done as good a job as my mother did for us.

Dad used to play a fancy red accordion, and a mouth organ, but for me he bought a Horn and Thompson Upright Grand Piano from Burton for £47. That was a lot of money in the '30s. I started music lessons when I was six years old.

At first I used to carry the music book under my arm, but it was so heavy I kept dropping it, and Dad said I'd got to keep my music nice and clean, so eventually, we went to Swad to buy a music case. It was fun looking in all the shop windows as we went up the High Street, and when we reached Mr. Wright's shop, and opened the door, a funny smell tickled my nose, and I wanted to sneeze. It was the smell of leather. On the shelves there were big suitcases and little ones, and lots of music cases as well. They all looked giant sized to me, and I didn't like the black ones, so Dad chose a brown one.

"You'll play better now you've got a music case, young lass," said Mr. Wright. I smiled at him, and wondered if I'd ever be able to play at all. There was such a lot to remember; all those notes for the right hand, and then some more to remember for the left, and as for playing on the black keys with both hands together, well! That was really hard.

Mr. Wright put the music case in a brown bag, Dad thanked him very much, and we went next door to the Candy Store. Outside, I stood chewing my favourite liquorice sweet, the round one with all knobbly things all over it, and liquorice in the middle. Dad had a plain black one, and reminded me to save a few for Mam. "Where are we going now, Dad?" I said. "We'd better be getting back, Topsy" (his favourite name for me.) I grinned at him and clasped his hand as we turned the corner to go down Midland Road.

At Scragg's the chemist, I stopped and looked in the window. They were still there on the shelves, four big fat round glass bottles with narrow necks, all full of different coloured liquid. "What's in the bottles, Dad?" I said, but Dad couldn't tell me, so we walked on until we came to the Milk Bar, where Dad must have read my thoughts.

When you were in agony with your teeth, your dad'd pull your tooth out. My dad used to say, "Loosen it up today at school." And you'd be groaning all day. When you got home, dad'd get a handkerchief and he'd twinkle it round a bit and then he'd pull it out. If it was a fairly loose one, he'd put a bit of cotton around and pull like that. You'd be there panicking, and he'd be trying to distract you and all of a sudden, there'd be a quick yank and it'd be gone.

"Come on, Topsy, we've got time for a drink," he said, so we went in. "Can I have a milk shake, Dad?" I said, and he lifted me on to the high stool at the bar, and I sat there with a straw in my glass, and all pink froth round my lips. Dad wiped it off before we got on the bus.

At home, I was eager to show Mam my new music case. "Let's have a look then," she said, as Dad put it on the table. "You'll look all posh now when you go for your lessons." Mam put the music book in the bag, and gave it me to hold. I'm sure she was trying not to laugh, because it was nearly as big as me, and it never wore out, even after nine years of music lessons and exams, with Mrs. Harrison, who lived down Swadlincote Road.

I used to go to Sunday School three times every Sunday, and they had Anniversaries every year. They got these 'ere planks to build a stage up round the pulpit, for the kiddies to stand on for singing, and a choir behind them. In those days they used to pump the organ with a handle. In Hastings Road where I lived, there was a little chapel just across the road, and we went there from very young ages. Me mother'd tell us we had to go to the chapel on Sunday morning and Sunday afternoon and possibly in the evening. We used to sit round in groups and have little stories told, and then we'd sing hymns and we'd have a nice little chat, and I can well remember signing the pledge when I was nine years old. I've still got it. It was a pledge to be teetotal. 'Water is best,' it says on it. It shows you on it, a maiden carrying a couple of buckets of water from the well. 'Water is best and I shall not drink,' and I had to sign that.

When me elder brother left school, he used to play the organ for the chapel, and I used to go pumping it up for him, me and me brother, and it was so old and dilapidated, the bell as'd got holes in, and we had to pump ever so hard to keep enough wind in so it played the organ. That was really hard work. You couldn't do it yourself, you had to have two of you and while you had a rest, t'other one was pumping away. If me brother was playing loud it took a lot of wind in and we had to pump faster.

We always looked forward to the Anniversary times about May time. The superintendent used tell us, "Now then, it'll soon be Anniversary time. We want you here for practice," and three or four times in the evening, we used to have to go for practice to learn the songs and the hymns and that, that we were going to sing on the platform, and we used to be thrilled to bits with it.

I remember going down to Darklands ash tip everyday after school to find old bike parts to make our own bikes. I have never had a decent bike to this day.

The man who took us was a chap named Freddy Boss. He were the conductor, call him what you may. When you first started practising for Sermons, you had boys one night and girls another night. An' then, towards the end, getting nearer to the Sermons, the boys and girls would join in, so that the sound was there. He'd jump off his bike, without going home for any tea, after eight or nine hours down the pit, and come straight into Chapel and take us lads, which, were no mean feat, I mean, there wasn't just half a dozen men, there were twenty or thirty lads and we wonna the easiest people to get along with! The South Derbyshire accent can be very broad. He used to say "Don't sing *to*, lads sing *too*, it sounds much nicer." To this day, in the choir I think about him. He was a real brick.

When the actual day came, we'd get our new clothes and went strutting up the platform, which used to hold about eighty at that time. Folks used come from all round to the Sermons. We used to think it was wonderful to see the chapel so packed with people, and even having to put chairs down the aisles, 'cause they hadn't got enough seats. They wouldn't allow that today, because of the fire hazard.

My mother used to pay into Salt's Club. Twelve shillings it were, and they used to have tickets, and tek 'em to Salt's. Mother bought all our Sermons clothes with 'em, and you only wore 'em on Sunday. We'd have a suit, shirt, tie, and a pullover, and you had to make 'em last till next Sermons. That was the only time you had new clothes, 'cause they couldna afford a lot in them days.

With us being lads, we generally had a blazer and trousers and when we were younger, white ankle socks and sandals. On the first day, on the morning of the Sermons, you went in, on the platform, in your last year's clothes. And you didn't put your new clothes on until the afternoon and evening, as there used to be three services in them days. But the afternoon and evening was the best attended service. I suppose for one thing, the mums were at home getting Sunday dinner ready, and it always used to be a bit of a scoot round on Sundays.

I remember one Sunday that I really put the family in a mess. I'd gone home from morning service and we'd had our dinner. We'd all changed. Mum said, "Now, right, while I get cleared up here you can go down to Swad Park." Me brother was always put in charge of us. Where there's a bit of a bowling green and tennis courts now, there used be a duck pond, what we always called Theaker's duck pond. There was an old tyre on the water and me and me brother were throwing stones at it. Well, I forgot to let go and

'In those days, when you went on the Chapel treat to, for example, Alvaston Park, or Sutton Coldfield, you used have to pay threepence, so I remember one year, there were said, "There's a big surprise coming off at the Chapel, so we all sat on the concrete road down Princess Street there, at Castle, and Billy Hales's Dad came round. Master Hale, and I said to him, "What's the big surprise Master Hale?" and he says, "You're getting your threepences back." Every hat went up in the air you know, because threepence was a big price then.'

went in, in me best clothes that I'd never had on before. I was not so much wet as sludged. And, of course me brother, when he took me back home, he just took me to the gate and let me go in on me own, with me Dad shouting at him through the window, "You wait till you come here." You know. But of course I had to go back on Sermons in the afternoon in me old clothes, 'cause, I'd ruined, well I hadn't ruined them, but they were in no fit condition to go to Sermons in on the afternoon. But I often think that it must have been a worry to me Mum, after she'd saved for twelve months to put you in something decent for the Sermons and then I go and jump in a pool of sludge, which it virtually was.

Me dad used have a load of coal delivered and when I used get home from school at dinner time, me mum would say, "Your dad inner getting that in when he comes home," so you got a ton of coal in before you went back school. You had a wash, and a bit of bread was shoved in your hand and you went back school eating your bread and jam.

Most miners liked a drink of beer but on a Sunday morning, you'd see them helping their wives with the breakfast and they'd have a wash and a shave and then they'd go and look at each others' pigs. We lived down Linton Heath and there were ninety-seven colliery houses in a row all down one side, and they'd start out at the top and they'd look at his pig and they'd guess how big it was…twelve score, twenty score or whatever. When the war came, they used to feed these pigs and they used to feed one for the Ministry and one for the house, so they could get meal quotas.

On a Sunday night, Mrs Jackson up at Princess Street 'er'd have no dominoes and 'er'd have no pianos going at all and all the men used be in their Sunday best, caps on there, sitting round. Of course, I was getting a bit older then and in a newspaper, it'd been on about going up to the moon and 'er says, "I dunna reckon they'll go up to the moon, dun yo," and they said to 'er, "ask young Ron there." And I said, "Yes, they'll probably go in my lifetime but not in your lifetime."

"Are you certain?" "Yes, I'm certain." "You can only be certain of two things in this life my lad, death and rent day." And they're right an all ant they!

A pig were almost like a vehicle in them days. It'd got to be licensed. The Ministry knew where every pig was that ever existed. As soon as you had a litter you had to register it. They'd do spot checks on you to see if you were hiding them. You were allowed to keep some yourself and the others had to be sold. The idea was to keep them until they were a prime weight and you'd get the maximum money for them. There was always a black market. The local bobby used to know all about pigs that the Ministry didn't know about. You'd give him a pound of bacon to keep his eyes shut. You used to hang a pig in the house and you'd salt it too. Used to have big sides of it and in fact, right up to the day we left the house, everytime we wallpapered, you could see this grease stain that'd come through, where the pig had hung on the side. Me dad'd say, "D'ye want a bacon butty?" and he'd reach over and cut a chunk off.

All this was prior to the NHS and you'd often have to pay for your medicines 'in kind.' I know a lot of our bills was paid in kind, with the doctor coming over and he'd be paid with a slice of bacon or a ham. We did alright - a slice of bacon got you a lot of treatment. It was the only way you could survive. Strictly speaking it was criminal but you weren't trying to do anybody down.

Bath time when I was little was nothing like it is today. We didn't have a bathroom or hot running water. There was just a cold tap in the scullery which was next to the back door. In the tiny scullery was a big brown sink with a curtain round it to hide the buckets, ladle, soap and soap powder, a box with shoe polish and brushes, furniture polish, brasso, bleach, disinfectant, floorcloth, dustpan and brush. The dolly tub and posher stood in the corner and on the side was a gas stove and big copper. A fire had to be lit under it after it was filled with water. My Mum always said you couldn't spin a cat round in our scullery and it was cold in there. In the kitchen we had a blackleaded fire grate with an oven on one side and a boiler on the other. Around the hearth was a brass fender you could see your face in and a companion set stood on the hearth with coal tongs, brush shovel and poker, and a big range, also with a brass top. I used to love polishing it. Saturday was bath night so we all was nice and clean for Sunday School at the chapel. Dad would light the fire under the copper and the parlour fire as well, if the weather was cold. He would then put a big sheet of brown paper down on the carpet in the parlour and then bring in the large galvanised bath which hung on a hook on the outside lavatory wall in the back yard. Mum used to give it a good wipe out with an old rag and some carbolic soap.

Then Dad would ladle the water out of the boiler and the copper into a white enamel bucket and fill the bath up. He filled the copper and boiler up again with cold water ready for wash day on Monday morning. When all was ready I would go in the bath first; being the only girl, I didn't get as dirty as the boys and anyway they usually played football and cricket. If they were really muddy, Dad would rub them down first in the scullery with a soapy flannel and warm water in a bowl in the sink, while I was having my bath. We didn't have bubble bath, shower gel or shampoo, just Lifebuoy soap or Fairy or Palmolive. But it was lovely. After Mum had rinsed me down with a ladle of clean water she would wrap me in a big towel and rub me dry. I then got into my pyjamas, dressing gown and slippers and would go through into the kitchen while the two boys used to go in one at each end or so they tell me. I never saw them undressed; we led quite a sheltered life in them days. After the boys had been bathed and dressed in their pyjamas, Dad would take in some more hot water and top the bath up for Mum and Dad was last to go in. He then had the laborious task of emptying the bath. We had a front door in the parlour so he'd ladle it out into the bucket and water the front garden when the water had cooled down and wash the path, window sill and door step as well and then wipe out the bath and hang it up on the hook on the lavatory wall until next week.

I remember me mother used to say in those days, we all pulled together, and it's true, we did. One night me mother said, "I'm locking you lads in tonight, while I go over to Mr. Perry's. He's got pneumonia, and he's on the change." There was a change in pneumonia. They used to poultice them then, and they'd sit up all night.

Mrs. Perry would often come in from next door and she'd say, "Lizzie, I've made too much stew, and there's some taters here, would your lads like 'em?" "They would," said me mam, and she'd tell us to sit down, and we got 'em straight away, no messing.

Sometimes me mother would hold the bread to her breast when her cut it then er'd dig into the old margarine and saw us off a big noggin, and er'd flip it across the table to us. Then we'd get a big bottle of Daddies sauce and spread it on the bread, and away we went.

On Saturday nights we had a bath in front of the fire, and me mother always gave us lads a cup of senna when we got out. It had four or five senna pods in, it was a laxative you see.

Me dad had the meat 'cause he was a worker, and I can see him now, before Gresley Baths opened, when he washed himself. We used have a big bath, and me mother used to get it on the hearth, and he used to kneel down and wash himself, and when it was cold, me mother used to tek the oven shelf out, and wrap it in some flannel, and shove it in the bed, and we'd put our feet on it as lads. She also used to save the hen fat, and rub

Sometimes when you went up the garden you would meet a little stocky man wearing a bowler hat and he had just flushed your toilet. I found out that it was Mr. Pollard, the Sanitary Inspector from the Council. Only a few years earlier the sewerage system had been installed in the area. He was just seeing if it was working all right. Mr. Pollard became a sort of Bogie Man to us children. If you had done anything wrong you would be reported to Mr. Pollard. That was the only really leg pull to make you behave yourself.

it on us chests. In summer we used go blackberrying, and she used mek blackberry vinegar, and if we caught a cold, she'd rub the hen fat on us, and give us a glass of blackberry vinegar to drink. That was all we had.

Every week me mother would get us to kneel on the floor against her knees, and 'er'd look in your hair with a fine toothcomb for nits. It were a regular thing. She always used say, "Who are ya sitting against at school?"

Me dad pegged rugs as well, and he cobbled for us lads. We used watch him a'front of the fire, and there used be a gas light on top of him, and he had all the tacks in his mouth, and then he'd hit his fingers, and he used say, "If you lot go sliding in these boots again!" We used to hide under the table when he'd got his hair off! He used to do all them things, and they seemed to have a lot more time to do it than we have nowadays.

I lived in a little row of cottages against the Drum and Monkey because my Dad worked at Gresley Pit. We lived in a Moira Colliery House, and it was there I went to the Get Wisdom School at Gresley. Mrs Woodrow was the Headmistress and there was a Mrs Wibley that came from Linton. George Holmes' wife taught me in the Infants, and Miss Swindale and then another lady, a Mrs. Harvey who married one of the Cartrights - builders at Woodville, and there was a lady in the top class who was called Miss Trot: she came from Belper, that's a proper Belper name.

A lot of people have forgotten we had a British Empire in those days, and we had an Empire Day. We used to put the flag outside and we all had to salute this flag.

The vicar Despar came from Gresley and his wife, and we used to have a sing-song. You never hear it sung nowadays.

> *Brightly, brightly songs of Spring. Upon this happy day,*
> *Shine upon us as we sing, this 24th of May.*
> *Shine upon our brothers, far across the ocean blue,*
> *As we raise this song of praise, on this glorious Empire Day.*

We didn't get a certificate on Empire Day, but we used to get one on health weeks. If you used to wash your hands in Lifebuoy soap, teacher used to put a star in a book. It was okay at the Get Wisdom School. I didn't get much wisdom though. I realised that when we were done at Castle Gresley Central School. We were a long way behind those from Linton. They had had more than us.

My broad South Derbyshire accent began to show itself as I grew up starting with the day I began school at the age of five. There was no way I was going to leave my celluloid duck floating in a tin bath in the garden, without me there to push it, so I stood in the middle of the road, hands on hips and said to Mum, who'd been dragging me along up to then, "I anna goin' school, an' ye canna mek me!" She did though and for a five year old, a clip around the ears wasn't much fun. We played a sort of tug o' war game all the way up to the school - she pulling me and me holding back. I wasn't going to give up without a struggle. Anyway, once I was there, I quite enjoyed it. I liked colouring books and drawing things but I still couldn't wait to get back home to my celluloid duck. After that first day, I went to school without having to be persuaded.

At one time while living in a small terraced two up, two down cottage in Jail Yard, I only had boys as playmates and so I became what was known then as a bit of a tomboy. I loved climbing trees and one day, I was about to climb my favourite oak tree in the field at the bottom of the garden, when an old lady saw me and said, "Tha munner do that ma duck, tha'll 'ert thee sen!" I climbed down, muttering as I ran, "Er'll not stop mai climbin' traze." I soon learnt that Monday was always 'Weshdee' and Saturday night was a night out at the 'pictures' in Swad. Sometimes the conversation with the neighbours would go like this, "Are you goin' pictures tonate?" "No, we anna goin' tonate, it's too code." My broad South Derbyshire ended abruptly at the age of nine in 1943. The Second World War was in its fourth year and we had evacuees over from London and before you could say, "Cor, luv a duck," I was speaking like a Londoner.

We had to walk to school in those early days, and at Belmont Street School, Swadlincote, the day began with morning assembly in the school yard, after the bell had gone at 9 o'clock. The children formed lines in the school yard, under the watchful eye of one of the teachers (who took it in turn) and the children marched in an orderly fashion to the various classrooms.

In the class, the register was read out, and the children answered "Here, Miss" or "Present, Miss" in response to their names being called. We didn't have a special uniform to wear.

In the morning, each child whose mother could afford $2\frac{1}{2}$d a week (which hardly computes in today's money) was given a small bottle of milk to drink.

We learned reading, 'riting and 'rithmetic, as it was known back then. Geography and history were taught, and we did drawing and painting, but there were no facilities for woodwork, so we all had to walk to Newhall School for that. We did P.T. in the playground, that's physical training, like bending, stretching, arm swings, running and jumping, and we had to do it whether it was cold or not, well, we didn't have a gymnasium you see, or a swimming pool.

We had religious education, which taught us right from wrong, but like all kids, we still scrumped a few apples, and played a few pranks in class, like flipping a rolled up piece of paper off a ruler on to somebody's neck, but we sometimes had to pay for our little pranks, because the cane was used in those days. It was six of the best on each hand. On the whole, Belmont was a good school, keen in their efforts to give us a good education and a good start in life.

We played games in the street after school. Ball games like rounders using the flat of the hand to hit the ball, and as we ran to the den, only the bowler was allowed to hit a person to catch them out before they reached the den. The other fielders had to throw at the den, which was usually someone's jacket or knitted pullover, placed on the ground. In winter we used to go looking for conkers in the woods, which we hung on a piece of string and held in mid-air while another boy would do his best to break the conker, by hitting it with his own. Then we would see whose conker would last the longest.

Holloways was a big canvas tent and they used to do Maria Marten and Sweeney Todd and that sort of thing. As kids we used sort sneak underneath the flap of the tent and watch it free until we was found out and then we were chucked out. Anyway it was amateurish but it was good.

O.U.T. spells out

Another game we played was holler,
When you shout it's called a holler,
You know, hollerin, like.
And we would play holler,
and two or three go off up the road and hide, you see,
and the other would find them
and we used to shout
"Sound yer holler!"
So if I went to somebody
and they thought I shouted
"Sound yer holler!"
they would shout
"Squeak-if-yer-near!"

One lad who had been 'on'
stood with his head against the lamp,
like that,
and then you got picked,
you know.

I draw a snake upon thy back
Who finished it?
And they'd have to pick
who finished it.
And if they picked the right man,
that lad'd be 'on'.

Up a pole,
Down a pole,
Monkeys chew tobaccer,
How much did it cost?
Three pence.

In those days, there was hardly any traffic on the roads and us children'd play whip and top or football - all in the road - probably having to stop occasionally for a horse and cart coming down the street to empty a ton of coal outside a house. When it'd been emptied, all the neighbours would come an' help you get it in.

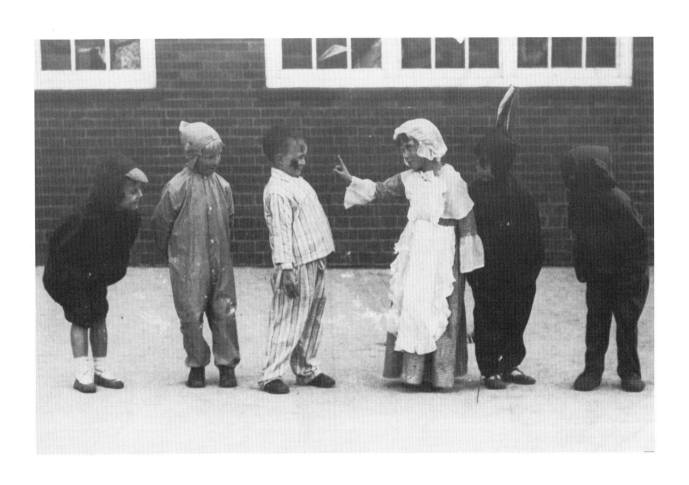

Penny, tuppence, threepence.
Well that lad was 'on'
you see.
But my favourite was:
Blib, blob
Snotty gob.

And sometimes
In the wintertime we'd play
tin-can-a-lurkey.
We'd have a tin can
and we'd put it somewhere,
and anybody who was picked,
if you could get to that tin can
before the lad that was 'on'
and throw it away again,
he was 'on' again,
you see.

But we used to go and get
a case ball,
a football.
My brothers and me,
in the wintertime,
we'd go blackberrying
and sell 'em and buy
a caseball
for winter, you know.
At the bottom of Cappy Hill
there was a shop there,
a pork butcher's shop,
where we'd go for a pig's bladder
and we'd blow it up
and play football with that.

Nothing seemed to happen regarding street games until Easter and Pancake Day. Then whips and tops were fetched out. Whips were fitted with a new boot lace or if you were lucky, a leather one which lasted much longer. There were three general types of top: Big Ben, where patterns were chalked on and they spun more slowly, Monkey Tops, which were hard to use as they soon fell over and more skill was needed and finally, the Window Breaker, and with this, you had to be a good runner as it was known to have flown ten yards from some whips, hence its title due to inadvertent breakages! As the weather warmed, more static games were played like snobs, marbles and skimming cigarette cards. Whoever knocked down the card leaning against the wall picked up all the cards on the ground.

The girls played hopscotch in carefully chalked courts and skipped to old rhymes repeated year after year without change. "O.U.T. spells out!" and the rope would be speeded up until it was a whistling blur and the legs could no longer keep up the pace.

Most of the lads' fathers would have a go at making a kite. Some were primitive but flew and some of them were decorated masterpieces which crashed miserably to the ground and were towed about until they turned back to the original sticks and paper from which they began.

I am sure there are many games that I have forgotten as they seemed to fill the year until the dark nights came and the lamplighter came to light the gas lights in the street.

In those days, your apples came in a barrel and these barrels had got two hoops around them about the size of a chair. My Mam used to get them two hoops and fasten them together so that you'd got a ring. One went this way and one went that way and my Mam used to tie them with a bit of string when she got cracking and bind them all the way around with crêpe paper and hang little ornaments on them with a little sprig of mistletoe in the middle. It would be hung up there when people came in the door. It was prettier than any Christmas tree.

Years ago, people used to make their own entertainment, like the travelling players called 'Mummers' who would set up their own tent on the village green. They had their own costumes for whatever drama they were going to enact and the charge to sit and watch was only in pennies. The village would buzz with excitement whenever they came. Youngsters in Swadlincote and villages round about, used to go from house to house doing a bit of 'guisering' to make some pocket money in the winter. It was like a one act play that they did, in costume, but they had to make do with whatever they could put their hands on - a sword for King George, for instance, would probably be formed out of a piece of wood, and a crown out of an old tin can. They'd wear pit boots, any old clothes, coats turned inside out and, of course, soot was spread everywhere, usually on their hands and faces.

The words were not written down, but they were passed down, and the parts in the play were usually passed from father to son, brother to brother, or even friend to friend. That's how the continuity went. Most of those that went guisering would be about thirteen or fourteen years old basically, and they'd rehearse outside in the wash house or any spot really, but usually in the wash house at the back of the houses, and of course with no electric lights, they'd have to have candles and they'd practise their play until they were more or less word perfect. Then by about the second week in December, they would start their rounds.

We used to go guisering when we were lads, me two brothers and I. We used to dress up, and act out a short play. For instance, King George had a wooden sword, and probably a crown, or something like that. The one who played the Doctor had his Dad's bowler hat on, and a pair of old glasses and an attaché case. Beelzebub had a dripping pan, and a club, and then there was Jack, the one who gets killed, and that was it. We used to have to go into the house like this. We'd knock on the door and go straight in, and with me being the youngest, me brothers used to shove me in. I'd be about eleven or twelve, something like that and I was the 'enterer'.

On one occasion, they shoved me in, and I opened this door, and said, "And then to enter in, to see what favour I can win," and the old chap of the house said. "Well, bloomin' well get out again, you anner comin' in 'ere." At any rate, I was first in, and I had to say, "I open this door and enter in, to see what favour I can win. Whether I stand or whether I fall, I'll do my duty to please you all." Then there'd be the following 'script':

"A room, a room, a gallant room. A room to let me in. Poke up the fire, and strike a light, for in this room there'll be a fight. I've acted once, I've acted twice. I've acted on the public stage. And if you don't believe the words I say, here comes Beelzebub to clear the way." In steps King George, and he says, "Let's have a fight!" They have a fight and Beelzebub drops to the floor, and he says to him, "What have you done? You've killed me only son Jack. Can there be a doctor found?"

"What kind of doctor? Will it be a £5.00 doctor?" "No!" "A £10.00 doctor?" "No!"

On the black range was a huge stewpan, which must have held four or five gallons of water and mixed vegetables which Grandad had grown in the garden. On odd times, when funds allowed, Grandma would send to Simpsons, the butchers, at the top of Stanhope Road, and buy a sheep's head for about 4d and into the pot it went. I used to come running home from school and say, "What's for dinner, Grandma?" She would turn from the pot and say, "Mountain pecker today, my lad." When I looked in the pot, there rising and falling, as it bubbled among the vegetables, with its bright green teeth and sad eyes, and its tongue hanging out, was the sheep's head. A meal fit for any prince.

"A £15.00 doctor?" " No!" "A £20.00 doctor?" "Yes!" and clapped his hands. Then in steps a £20.00 doctor. "What are your travels?" he says. "Italy, Sicily, France and Spain. And over the hills to Merry old England again." "Can you cure that man?" "If there's nineteen devils in that man, I can guarantee to fetch twenty out!" So, he gets twenty out. The old doctor gets on his knees, and gets his medicine bottle out of the attaché case.

"Here, Jack, drink out of this bottle, and let it trickle down thy throttle. When you feel it touch thy brain, arise, Jack, and fight again!" Jack rises up and he says, "What's the matter? My heart is confounded, I must be away!" And then we used to say, "Put out your table, and spread on it a cloth, we want some of your mouldy cheese, and some of your Christmas Log!" Then we took the hat round. You could find gangs of lads, getting on the bus from Linton to Swad, and doing it in the pubs. We weren't always welcome, but that was how it was. Me brothers would decide where we went and we shared what we got amongst us.

Days out

It was high summer and all the children were on school holidays. There were no seaside holidays in those days and six weeks seemed to drag on forever. So small parties of friends used to go for walks. The cry used to echo across the gardens, "We're going a walk along the bottom," as we used to call Hearthcote Road, and friends used to meet at the front of their houses and set off down the road.

Stanhope Road at this time of the year was alive with house martins and I mean scores of them, wheeling, soaring and diving with shrill cries: all the children used to call them 'Jack-Squealers." We would walk to the bottom of the road and then there would be a discussion about the route. Eventually some of the children would break off in a different direction, but the day about which I am writing concerns Darklands Road. We would walk by the side of the long brick wall which fenced off The Grove. Some of the older children said someone 'posh and wealthy' lived there, but none of us knew exactly who.

Opposite the wall on the other side of the road were what we called Wardy's fields. There were some old gas-tarred wagon sheds in the top corner for Mr. Charles Ward had a bakery and cake shop and also a funeral business. He had a shelabier with cut glass windows to carry the coffin to Gresley Cemetery, pulled by two black horses with plumes of black feathers fastened to the top of the bridle. They were driven by a small man named Bill Shakespeare, who wore a long black coat and a large top hat. Even the horses' hooves were done over with black boot polish.

Further down the road we came to the Fire Station and we used to scramble up the doors to look through the glass windows at the gigantic, gleaming red and polished brass Dennis Fire Engine.

We walked and talked along the way, for without any doubt, everyone knew our ultimate destination was the Catholic Church and Father Deegan's monkeys, which were kept in a pen in the corner of the churchyard.

First we crossed over Browny Brook and had a discussion leaning over the rails about the colour, which was a thick yellowy brown. Some said finally "it's ochery water, that's what that is," ochery being derived presumably from ochre, i.e. yellow ochre and so ended the discussion. We walked slowly up the hill, past Claudie Parker's lorry yard and finally reached our destination. Although we were scruffy and very poorly dressed, we were all greeted and smiled upon by Father Deegan. We all enjoyed the antics of the monkeys, waved goodbye to them and then slowly walked down home to see if there was any tea.

An old ochery brook
runs alongside a there.
It came from the old fish pond,
through the paddling pool,
straight down alongside
the old tramsheds,
and came out where Holts
had got a tip in a hole,
and it ran right down to Stanton
that ochery brook did.

One of the happenings to brighten the summer was the Co-op Treat. It was held at the Sandholes Field at Springfield Road. It came out of the surplus profits when all the members had drawn their 'divi' as they used to call it. It was not much by today's standards, just sandwiches and orangeade, served in the open air, with a Punch and Judy Show and one year I remember seeing some hot air balloons. Nothing like the ones seen today. These were made of tissue paper, on a light wooden framework, about one foot in diameter. There was a solid fuel burner underneath and they floated away merrily, but had a habit of bursting into flames. When they did, all the kids cheered because most of us thought that's what they were supposed to do.

The grand finale came when the women hurled boxes of sweets into the crowd of yelling and screaming children. A rough rugby match ensued and hands were stamped upon and hair pulled. I think some of us liked the hair pulling and finger stamping better than the sweets, but everyone managed to get a few to take home. So the day of the Co-op Treat ended with satisfaction to all, and Grandma said, when I arrived home, "Get to that sink, my lad, you're all mucked up!"

Half a century ago, I spent a good deal of time on Eureka Park. In those days, the swings and roundabouts were at the lower part of the park close to the tram shed and railway line. The path from Belmont Street passed under the railway with the bridge

'From time to time the Sherwood Foresters Band used to play in the Bandstand. They were very popular, and the park was crowded with people dancing around the bandstand to the music. When the time came for them to go to the park, they assembled on the road outside, and set off, trumpets blowing, and drums beating. One day, the band had assembled ready to march to the park, and my father Charles Arthur Bailey, bet Jim that he couldn't throw the mace over Gurdy Bridge and catch it the other side, whilst marching under the bridge, but Uncle Jim won the bet, and Dad had to buy him a pint.'

being so low that an average sized adult had to duck his or her head to get under it. One of my favourite roundabouts was know as the "Bobby's Button". This was a wooden roundabout about 3 ft high, 10 ft diameter and octagonal in shape. Metal rails radiated from the centre to the eight corners. At the bottom of the "Button" was a shelf or running board and one could get hold of a rail and run as fast as one could and then leap onto the shelf. Children could sit on the equipment while their parents stood and pushed the "Button" as the rails came round and this kept the momentum going.

Another favourite was the see-saw. This consisted of a wooden plank suspended from a metal frame by metal arms so that it could swing to and fro and the height of the plank above the crown rose at each end of the swing and low at the middle. Along the plank were metal handles placed at regular intervals for children's safety. The swings and mountain glide were much the same as they are today. All these amusements were very much used, with children running from one to another with a great deal of shouting and laughter.

Another great attraction was the paddling pool. This has now been filled in and a rose garden created. The water for the pool was provided by Midway Fishponds and arrived at the pool down a series of tree and shrub-lined cascades. I suspect that nowadays this would not conform to Health and Safety Executive regulations. The pool was oval in shape and shallow at the inlet end, only deep enough to allow paddling. But at the outlet it was deep enough for swimming. All round the pool was a shelf about eighteen inches down which could be used as a step to enter the pool or for young children who could paddle round in very shallow water whilst holding their parent's hand. Older children had a wonderful time splashing about in the deeper water, ducking and chasing each other. It was a good opportunity to be scantily clad on warm summer days. Park benches surrounded the pool, providing comfort for parents as they supervised the safety and behaviour of their young charges.

Between the pool and Newhall Road was a lawned area. This was always very well maintained with grass kept to a uniform length by regular mowing. Several beds of roses an mixed plants had been cut out of the lawn and a path round the perimeter. This path passed underneath several wooden arches supporting rambler roses, old favourites such as *American Pillar*, *Excelsior* and *Dorothy Perkins* being grown, which flowered magnificently during mid-summer. Between the path and the hedge was an informal border of shrubs and bedding plants. The 'piece de resistance' of this lawned area, however, was a most beautiful floral clock skilfully planted in intricate detail with hundreds of plants. The clock accurately told the time thanks to a mechanism under the flower surface and visitors travelled long distances to see this clock, such was its fame and beauty. What would surprise younger people was that all lawned areas had "Keep off the Grass" signs, which request was generally observed as was "No Cycling". There was also a shelter containing seats in this area, for the convenience of visitors, with toilets attached.

Almost all public parks at that time boasted a bandstand and Eureka Park was no exception. It was situated in the middle of the park and was a circular, wrought iron construction. The ironwork was elaborate and always gaily painted and seating was provided on the hillside adjacent, making a natural grandstand. As usual in mining areas brass bands were always a popular attraction and there was also a vogue for accordion bands.

Eureka Park has always boasted a first class bowling green which is remarkable when one realises that the Midland Road end was the site of the "Old Shoddy" Colliery whose spoil heaps covered that area. The remnants of the spoil heaps are now the present site of the swings. The mine shafts were in the grass area between the swings and the memorial gates. The bowling green was well provided for with seats for spectators and a border on two sides of shrubs and roses.

The field area was the venue for many events and large crowds gathered to witness them. This was the pre-television era and people expected to travel to these events for their entertainment. Literally thousands of spectators assembled to witness such events as athletic meetings and gymkhanas. Very few weekends went by without a gymkhana taking place. We would take sandwiches and "pop" for a cheap day out and if we were lucky we would be allowed to have an "okey". This was invariably that of Dythams, whose soft ice cream of this period was the best I have ever tasted. In 1948 I represented Newhall Junior School in the South Derbyshire Sports and had a memorable day, although I did not win anything. Everything was well run and most competitors friendly but I was amazed by the size of the crowd! I had not previously performed before such a large crowd.

It snowed and snowed the wintertime, years 46 and 7,
the drifts were deep and solid, for me it seemed like heaven.
We carolled with the Chapel, at Christmas, round our streets,
then slipped and crunched down garden paths, and old folk gave us treats.
Took crusts of bread for the ducks and birds that lived near the frozen pond.
Down through the wood, a silvery land, touched by a frosted wand.
Stood still as a stone, eyes popping wide, as creatures crept to be fed
heart beating fast, 'cos our Mam had said, "without us they'd be dead."

In 1929 the Lea Memorial Park was being built. During July of that year my school had a visit from one of the Council officials. He spoke to my class particularly as we were all ten year olds and he was asking for volunteers to work on the park during our August holidays. (These were only four weeks at that time.) Quite a few of us put our hands up, but he picked only four of the biggest lads. I was one of them and our wages were to be the princely sum of 10/- per week (50p). That was not bad because a working man's wage at that time was £2 - £3 per week. The hours were 8.00 a.m. - 5.00 p.m. Monday to Friday, 8.00 a.m. - 1.00 p.m. Saturday with a half hour break for dinner. One man was in charge of us and our first job was to weed the two bowling greens, the putting green and I think there was a croquet lawn as well. In all we enjoyed it, particularly as it helped money come into the family.

When the park was finally opened, the bandstand was in full use with various brass bands giving concerts every Sunday evening. This was much more popular that it would be today. In those days, radio had hardly got going, and not many people had sets. The only 'canned' music was the old acoustic gramophone with a horn, so hearing a real live band was something of a novelty and people really enjoyed it.

I had great times on the Common, which was down Market Street at Gresley. Well of course it wasn't a park then, it was where they used to tip all the breakage and tiles. We used go picking tiles off there. Lovely tiles and pots we used to go and pick them off. They were what Greens tipped. One of the best things of that time was a trip to Holloways' Travelling Theatre, sometimes called Holloways Blood Tub, because of the kind of plays they performed. They used to come about twice a year on the Common, with this great big tent, and we used to go up to see 'Maria of the Red Barn' and these blood thirsty murder things, you see. 'Course me Dad took me, he wouldn't let me go

'I was born during the First World War. I used to have fainting bouts and me mam said it was with carrying me, as she used to mither. The doctor said, 'She isn't like one of yours, Mrs Harrison, but she may alter when she's seven.' Anyroad I was a big worry to me mam as I'd only eat toffee and water. Me mother said, 'You needner bother, you'll have to go to hospital and have your belly cut open if you don't stop eating toffees!' But our Sissie, who was always one who made a fuss of us said, 'You wonner have to go to hospital.' Anyroad, I started taking stuff off me dad's plate and looking up at him and me mother used to pile his dinner up so that she could get it down me. That's how I started eating.'

alone. It always used to be full. You had to pay. I don't think it was very expensive, but by gosh they used to queue up to go, and they used to have sessions in the afternoon, sessions at night, sometimes two or three.

They used to have stalls and fried chips. Oh yes, you'd get a pennyworth of chips, and ha'p'erth of chips in paper. When the big tent was there, they used to have them all round outside, and they used to sell fruit and stuff, shrimps and potatoes, and that sort of thing.

At the Fair up at Gresley Common, they used have a greasy pole and when I was a little lad I did quite a lot of climbing. When nobody was looking, I'd climb up the nearest lamp post and show the kids how fast I could climb. This particular time at the Fair, we saw this pole. I ran home and said to me mum, "Can I put me old trousers on?" and she said, "Yes, but why?" and I answered, "There's a greasy pole on the Common and there's a leg of lamb at the top and if anybody can climb it, and fetch that down, they can keep it." Well, I ran back to the Fair and me brothers were there and a few more friends and some more lads and I had a go but I didn't get anywhere near it. I only got about half way up and I kept slipping down. I was all covered with grease so I gev up the attempt and I kept thinking, "If only I could get that leg of lamb, I'd love to tek it for me mum," but I got nowhere near and I didn't see anybody else get it neither.

When the Fair used to arrive on the engine ground, Daredevil Peggy used to be one of the acts that opened the Fair, and closed the Fair, so before the stalls or the rides opened on the Fair this act would be performed. It's what's known nowadays as a high fire dive. The idea was that there was a tank which was roughly twelve feet in diameter, and six feet deep filled with water.

There was a tower put up sixty feet high with a short diving board off it and a ladder up to it. Daredevil Peggy only had one leg, but he would mek his way up the ladder to the diving board. He would have a suit on; something like an overall. Oil would be spread across the water in the tank. Peggy would douse himself in petrol or something similar. They would light the fire, so that the oil on the top of the water was ablaze, and then Peggy would light himself up, and within seconds, would dive sixty feet into the tank and put himself out, and the flames would be on top of the water.

That was the opening act of the Fair, and he'd do it again when it closed. His real name, I believe was Leslie Gadsby, and he'd been performing diving acts, and escapology

I could tell you a bit about what happened at the coconut shy with me and another lad. We lived up Nelson Street here at the time. We went to the Fair one night, and they had these twin sort of coconut shies, you know. We had four balls, and we put a tanner on this box and we got 'em. Well, we couldna knock 'em off with two wooden uns and we'd got some iron governors in us pockets, so he lets fly with iron governors, and knocks two off, and two more off, so I got up and knocked another two off each.

for quite a while, and would normally travel around the coasts with these acts, diving off piers, from Bangor round to Skegness. You used to have all kinds of bizarre acts - people being strapped to settees or chairs and thrown off the ends of piers and escaping from them!

The Fair came at Bank Holidays. They'd start putting the Fair up Friday, and go full blast Saturday and Sunday on those days, and probably Monday, the Bank Holiday and it would be all ready to pack up again. When you think that you didn't have things like T.V. and the only other entertainment was the two cinemas and the Rink, it was an alternative source of amusement, and they used to be absolutely packed. Dodgems and everything else, everybody had a bash at everything. The coconut shies was the thing, and you could see these big brawny miners knocking the coconuts off, and the trick was to hit 'em at the top, so you pushed the top off like that, so then they slid off. But even the fairground people were dead crafty, because they used to pack sawdust at the back. They were on stands and they used have a sort of cup shape at the back with the coconut stuck on the sawdust. But if you hit it properly at the top, the end would come off and it would roll off.

The dodgem cars were the main attraction for me, because as there were very few cars around, you'd got the chance to get behind the wheel of something, and the great delight was, you never went round, you spent your time ramming all and sundry, especially, if you reached the stage where you had a girlfriend, you'd have a bit of a show off.

Holland's Fairground had two traction engines that used to mek the electric juice. Their names were *Victory* and *Challenger*, and when they came to Swadlincote, they brought another one that drove the big ride horses. They also had the cake walk, and I remember as a lad, when Bishtons stood with a coconut shy there, and I went one night, and a chap said to me, "Shall you come and stand on coconut shy tonight, and shout six balls for a tanner". Yes, but what happened, my Dad and Mother came round, and I'd been in bed a month ill. What did me Dad tell me. "Get off home." Everyday, when I came home from school at Hastings Road, when the fairground were coming, I used to go and see what were coming fresh, and all that, because my Grandad used to stand with 'em, on the Brandy Snap Stall with Neilses.

Up to the Second World War breaking out, most villages and towns had Parades and Galas, and some were quite lavish with lots of decorated floats, numerous brass bands,

They'd be all decorated up with coloured bulbs and brass fittings. Every part of the paint work polished; puffing steam, and clouds of smoke coming from the stacks. The favourite ride at that time was the horse carousel. It had its own steam-driven organ, with drums, cymbals and other musical instruments. These marvellous machines had a sound all of their own.

stalls, tug-o-war, in fact, all sorts of things, but it all stopped while the war was on.

They used to have Parade and Galas up Woodville. My Dad organised that. We used to have the Derby Serenaders, and the Highlanders, and the Midshipmen, and all the bands used to come. The first one we had was Joan Parry. She was the Beauty Queen...

Woodville decided to hold its first Parade and Gala after the war had ended in 1949. I was fifteen, and came home from school one day, and Mum said: "Dad's entered you for the Gala Queen Contest of Woodville." "He hasn't," I said. "He has," said Mum, "and you've got to go to this place in Moira Road for the judging." "Judging?" I said. "How many's going?" "About a dozen or so," said Mum. 'Well,' I thought. 'What's Dad gone and got me into now!'

He was a good Dad really, and gave me anything I asked for, so I knew how disappointed he would have been if I'd thrown a tantrum, and said I wasn't going, so I let him teach me how to walk in a straight line with a book on my head. 'One foot in front of the other, that's the proper way,' he said, and he wrote a speech for me to practise (in case I won).

On the night of the judging, I wore my favourite blue crepe dress, with white flocked flowers all over it, and laced at the front, gypsy style. Washed my hair in Amami shampoo, and put on my new white canvas sandals with a bow on the front. Dad went up the road to the telephone box at the Rodney in Hartshorne, ordered a taxi from Mr. Ellis at Frederick Street, Woodville, and away we all went.

There were about twenty other girls from my school in this large room in Moira Road, Woodville, and I wasn't particularly nervous because I never thought for a moment that I'd win - but I did. There were four attendants chosen. Phyllis Scott, Rita Collier, Dorothy Ringham and Brenda Pickering. Also, two small girls, and two small boys. I've often wondered if the little ones still remember that day. Anyway, we all had to travel to Beamhill Road in Burton with Mrs. Parker (Bill and Wath's Mum) from Woodville, to have dresses made, and pageboy outfits for the boys in gold satin.

Two days before the gala, we all had to go to Swadlincote in the evening to a film premier at the Majestic Cinema. John Avery, then a young man, was the manager, and he looked so smart in his black evening suit, crisp white shirt and black bow tie. He took us all back stage and we changed into our new dresses for the Gala, and someone helped us to use stage makeup. It was a bit like Max Factor cake makeup, and the lipstick felt it had come out of the chip pan, all thick and greasy. On stage, I wasn't prepared for the

I think the first film I saw was Snow White and the Seven Dwarfs. That was at the Majestic, and I remember seeing Moira Shearer in 'The Red Shoes #' as a ballerina. I saw her because I'd been cooking at cookery that day at school, and I'd made a salad, and I know they had to bring me out in 'The Red Shoes', and I was sick in the Foyer, and John Avery brought me Salvalatoli.

bright footlights. I could hardly see into the audience, but maybe that was a good thing, because after being introduced as the Woodville Parade and Gala Queen with my attendants, John said that he hoped everyone would come to the gala on Monday, because the proceeds were for charity. He then escorted me to the black ebony piano and I played *The Rustle of Spring*, and *The Robins Return*. I was presented with a bouquet of flowers, and then we walked down steps that led from the stage, into the audience.

Can you imagine the excitement we all felt! As we reached the foyer, we heaved a sigh of relief, because everything had gone so well and then we literally ran up the stairs to join our parents already sitting on the front row of the balcony. I looked at Dad, and he smiled at me. He was thrilled. We all settled back to enjoy the film, but my mind was in a whirl, thinking about the Gala day to come.

On Monday, the Parade started about 1pm. It was a fine day, but windy, and we didn't have hairsprays back then, we had to rely on hairgrips to keep everything in place. The floats and the vehicle were adapted to carry the Queen, and her entourage, so we all made our way to John Knowles Sports Field in Woodville.

After the crowning ceremony by Mrs. Love, we walked round the field to wish everyone a happy day, and we stood for photographs to be taken by those in the crowd with cameras. The brass band contests were wonderful to watch. Breaston Highlanders in their swinging kilts and busbies, Derby Midshipmen in their sailor suits, and Derby Serenaders in their more exotic black outfits with flared trousers and sombrero type hats.

The whole day was a great success, and brought to a close by a dance at night. We attended many functions throughout the rest of the year, until it was time to hand over the crown to Brenda Pickering at the following year's Gala in 1950. The chosen Queen in 1951 was Rita Collier, and the Gala continued to be held each year after that until 1961.

When we were comin' home, we'd just shout, "Number 47, please," and you'd get off and then someone else would shout "Number 55," and they'd continue down the road, puttin' people off every twenty yards. That's what you call real service.

chapter two
The Heart of Swad

On the Delph

The bell on the town hall clock hardly stirs the town.
Yet as wisps of smoke from Sharp Bros drift along the street,
sounds begin to emerge.
Iron tyred wheels
and the sound of horses' feet
some trotting
others moving slowly
laden with goods.
The mumbling clack of the trains with their bells ringing.
Now hear the market vendors
each with their own personalities,
striving to catch hold of a customer and sell them something,
no matter how small
because money is tight and scarce.
It's Friday night.
The time when the magic of the market springs to life.
There's a forest of green tarpaulin tops
on the wooden stalls and each stall
has its own lamp.
I can smell them now,
the paraffin flare lamps,
pressurised by pumps fitted to the containers.
The hissing and the flaring from the naphtha flares.
They spit and fizz away
and you watch
as the unburned naphtha forms into little globules
falling over the stalls.
Fitful flames
momentarily lightening the darkness...

Pay Day. The Delph was crowded. Shoppers, kids in tow, pushed and shoved their way to the stall of their choice, stocking up for the week to come. I clutched my mother's hand even tighter as we were caught up in the crush, being propelled towards the fish stall of Lenny Blankley. This was the first time that I had been so close to him, a small, wizened, middle aged man with a rasping voice. The first time that I saw and heard him speak was one day on Commonside in Church Gresley at a memorial stone-laying ceremony shortly after joining the Gresley Boy Scouts. He started to shout and mimic us, frequently pausing to drink from a large bottle. During the week he sold fish from a flat-topped dray, pulled by a sleepy looking pony who seemed to instinctively know the way home when his inebriated master had finished his rounds. A rhyme we kids sung then was:

"Lenny Blankley, Lenny Blankley, Lenny Blankley sells fish.
Don't buy it, don't fry it. It sticks in the dish."

I wonder now if 'sticks' was the right word. It might have been 'stinks'.

Another travelling fishmonger was Mr Hextall. He sported a magnificent head of pure white hair and I believe wore shorts all the year round.

Mum would wend her way round and had eventually filled the big wicker basket with fish, meat and vegetables. I was steering her towards the confectionary stall in the market hall. Mum had informed me that the more expensive stalls, those 'specialising' as she put it, were to be found in the market hall. The traders had to pay more to hire the stalls but I suppose they passed the increase on to the customers. I asked her what the motto, 'Time the Avenger' over the clock meant. She looked pensively down on me as she told me that, at the end, the Great Reaper would judge us all. I was puzzled so asked the Vicar of Saint Stephens in Woodville what she meant. He smiled as he said that God was the judge but only the ungodly would be cut down. I was still confused.

The shouts from the vendors outside grew louder, "Ladies, come and look. You'll get no finer in the city and that's a fact - nor as cheap." We looked with the others but seldom bought. I finished eating the small chocolate bar mum had bought me, on the bus back to Woodville.

The year was around 1943. I was twelve, and a crowd of us were outside the *Mail* office, waiting for the papers to be delivered. I worked for Hallams, the newsagents, and we were hanging around waiting, and one of the lads produced a tennis ball and said,

"Shall we have a throw at the clock?"

He meant the one on the Town Hall at Swadlincote. It was dead opposite the *Mail* office then, and I said, "Arr, come on, we'll have three shots each, and see who can hit it first."

I had the first shot and missed, but on my third go I hit the clock. There was the sound of breaking glass, and a hole appeared in the clock. We ran off, and I hid in them toilets down Midland Road, where the new market is now, an' I stayed there. I was commonly known as Snowy then. Everybody knew me as Snowy, but me real name's George.

Me dad came home from work next morning, and I mean, he were a strict disciplinarian. There were three lads in the family for a start, so he'd got to be.

He walked in from Granville Pit, off nights, and his opening words to me mum were, "Blow me somebody's broke the Town Hall clock now!"

I sat there shaking in me shoes, and I didn't say anything, but at dinner I says to me mum, "Do you know who broke the Town Hall clock mum?"

"No, 'course I don't." "Well," I said, "I did it," and she gave me a look.

"You mustn't say that else you'll have the folk believing it."

I said to 'er, "It's true mum! but don't tell me dad." But she must have thought about it during the afternoon, and thought, "Well, if I don't tell him and somebody else does, it's going to be a darn sight worse that it is at the moment."

When I got home from school, me dad said, "You're going across to Chicky Whetton's with me ma lad."

I knew him as Mr Whetton, but me dad always called him Chicky Whetton. He was the supervisor or superintendent of the Town Hall.

Me dad took me across, and I had to tell him what I'd already told me dad.

"Right!" he said, "Meet me outside the council offices in Midland Road, in the morning at 9 o'clock.

"Well, I should go to school," I said.

"You'll have to get your mum or your dad to send a note to say that you can't come to school till the afternoon," he said.

Anyway, I went to the council offices, and I was taken before the engineer and surveyor, or whatever they called the head man then, and he gave me a lecture about playing with

a ball in the High Street, when we've got two perfectly good parks to play in, and then he said, "And whatever possessed you to throw at the clock?" and I said, "Well, I were under the impression it was just a wall I was throwing at - not glass, and I were as surprised as anybody when it broke," which I was.

"Well," he says, "It presents us with rather a quandary. Taking you to Court."

"But I didn't do it on purpose!" I said.

"Well," he said, ignoring my plea, "You see, the problem is - who to get to prosecute you. The Town Hall was raised by public subscription" (which it's got on the front now) "and the clock was given by Lord Gresley, on the understanding that they'd put underneath 'Time, The Avenger', so we can't get the public to prosecute you, and we can't get Lord Gresley, 'cause he's no longer here, so we're sort of left in this quandary."

Old Master Whetton said, "Well, I must say that this probably wouldn't have happened if the bomb hadn't been dropped on Baker Street during the war, as this caused the glass in the clock to crack. We knew it was cracked and of course all it needed was a tap to knock the piece out that were cracked." And then he said, "It's long been the discussion of the council to have the clock illuminated, which we daren't do before, because of the cracked glass, so now, it will probably be an opportune moment to have the glass replaced, and the clock illuminated."

So, Swadlincote owes me a little debt of gratitude for an illuminated clock.

At that time, me eldest brother was in the Pits as a Bevin Boy, and he were doing his trade at Cresswell Colliery, and they put a piece in the *Mail* about it in that Burtonians' Diary, and it said in there that - "A Swadlincote Boy Made the Town Hall Clock His Target For Tonight," and it said that after the third shot, he found he'd scored a hit!

Me mother cut the piece out of the paper and sent it to me brother, and he wrote back and said, "Wot's up, is our kid slipping? Why didn't he hit it first time?"

Following on from that, prior to me breaking the clock, me little brother had broken a windscreen on a council lorry, when they had the dustbin lorries. Me brother was in the garden at the time, and someone was throwing at him; he were only four, and he got fed up with it, and he picked a brick up and threw it back, but the council lorry moved forward and he hit the windscreen.

I know it were dangerous, it might have blinded the fellow who were driving, but me little brother were only four and he didn't know any better. The driver came round for me dad to pay for a new windscreen, and me dad said, "Pay for a bloomin' windscreen? We're having a job to live on my money as it is."

The Rev. Stevens approached Sir Henry de Vaux who was married to Sophia the widow of Sir Roger Gresley, and was living at Drakelow Hall. Sir Henry had already subscribed to the market hall fund, but Stevens returned to Drakelow to ask for further financial assistance. Sir Henry was in a bad mood. He was suffering from gout and had just lost a law suite; but finally agreed after being pressured by Stevens to find the provision of a clock, if the words Time the Avenger were placed underneath. He is reputed to have shouted "I'll beat those damn lawyers yet." The total cost of the market hall was £1,179 including £44 for the clock.

So the council suggested we pay so much extra money on the rent, and me dad agreed, but when he heard that I'd broke the clock, he said, "Are you trying to get us thrown out of the bloomin' house? We're having to pay for a windscreen, and now you'n gone and broke the clock!" and he was really up in arms about it.

But anyway, over the windscreen business, me dad knew Jack Staley, who was the rent collector, and me dad said to him, "How long have we got to keep paying this extra rent for the windscreen, Jack?" and Jack said, "Has anyone said anything to you Joe?" Me dad said, "No."

"Well, pack it up then," said Jack, "they'll let you know if they want any more."

Me dad just stopped paying it, and that's the saga of the clock.

The clock that keeps its eye
Day and night on the market place
Has the words 'Time the Avenger'
Inscribed like a smirk on its face
And in the hall underneath, the magistrate
Had you 'Under Swad Clock' if you didn't go straight.

I remember the time I was 'Under the Clock' at Swad. I was courting my now wife, Rose, at the time and she'd come over for a Sunday afternoon. I'd had a drink at dinner time in the White Lion and any road, I come up the road, and saw Rose's brother, he'd got a handchange motor bike and I says, "I'm thinking of having a motor bike, Don," so he said, "Try mine out."

So, I got on the motor bike and went up the road and I thought, 'This is alright.' Just as I got on the road, the police come by. He were reversing faster than I were going forward. The brother-in-law stood at the front with his motor bike tackle on, so the police came to me and said, "Could I see your licence please." I said, "You don't have to be a Sherlock Holmes to see what's happened here." Anyroad, I got a summons. No insurance, no driving licence, I'd got nothing. I'd only gone about ten yards on the road in it.

Well, I think all the Pit come Town Hall as they know'd I'd got a summons, and down the White Lion, they'd got a book down there with all the prices on, as how much I should get fined, and they were betting. The police were there an' all, in the book.

It wanna a policeman as I knew that come across in his car. It were another one, 'cause I used go shooting with these police round about the village and anyroad, they put the prices down as what it was and I got the summons come up.

There were me at the front and the brother-in-law. So this Sergeant Emery, I think were on the bench at the time from Linton. 'Cause Mrs Manners she used to do it, and they always reckoned as if Mrs Manners were on the bench and she'd got 'er 'at on, you got a stiff fine. But if 'er got 'er 'at off, you were alright. So, anyroad, this Emery said "Stand up, lads". We stood up at the front. He said, "Have you got a licence?" "No," 'cos this Banton had been in the witness box and said what had happened. He'd said to me at the time, "Everything you say you know, I shall put down in this book. I says "It's left to you now."

Well anyroad, I stood up. Emery said, "Have you got a licence now lad. I said "No", I said, "I don't think I'll bother with one." Well, if you'd have heard that Court! So he says, "I'm going to ban you from driving for twelve months and your brother-in-law Don. "But after six months," he says, "Apply for your licence and you'll get it back."

Well, I had to pay the fine. In fact, I've still got that little bit of paper now. That was first time I'd been in the paper. I got fined a pound. I'd no insurance. No driving licence. I'd got nothing, and the brother-in-law, he got fined ten shillings, I think it was. I went to the Sergeant and paid 'im, and I says, "Shall I be able to drive a car?" so he says, "I'll have to go and ask Mr Emery." He went to the back of the court and round. He says, "Oh yes," he says, "it's just for motor bikes." So I got banned, and after six months I applied for me licence. Then I had big motor bikes, and passed me test on them. Side cars, and then we started with cars. Everything's been alright since then, but it learned me a lesson.

I used to assist my mother occasionally on Saturday morning, my duty being to carry the heavy bags. Her modus operandi was to walk down the street pricing up the goods in which she was interested and purchase on the way back, having decided where the best value was to be had. All the grocery shops took a great pride in this window's display and much time and effort was put into making an attractive window as this was the bait to tempt potential customers in.

What would surprise today's shoppers would be the small size of the premises of these national companies. With the exception of the Co-op in West Street, which had large departments, they were small and the Maypole was tiny. There was floor space for

about half a dozen customers and if they had a line in stock that was generally in short supply, a queue soon formed which spilled out into the street. These shops were all organised in the same way, the staff behind the counter and goods for sale on the counter or on shelves on the wall behind the counter. All purchases had to be brought to the counter by the assistant, self-service was a long way into the future. The price of the goods were very often totalled on the back of a paper bag and only the final total put on the till. It was usual on the market and in small shops for the shopkeeper to total up the bill mentally.

An additional duty for staff was to cut out or cancel the necessary points out of your points book for items on ration. If you had used your points for that period you could not have the commodity. This was to guarantee that everyone got a fair share of scarce goods.

When I was only fifteen, just left school, me dad got me a job at Liptons' handling all the ration books. Nylons were really short in those days so the girls from the shop used to send me to the market on Saturdays to queue for their nylons and they wouldn't believe I wanted eight pairs and I'd need each girl's signature as proof. Even jellies were rationed and very rare. The people you had the ration books for had first choice of everything after the rations and the boss said, 'I've got a nice surprise for you girls but don't tell anybody! We've got some jellies but keep them under the counter, just give one to your best customers and say to them, "I've got a little present for you." It was just like you see on Dad's Army where they'd have an odd sausage and it'd be like, "I've put you a nice little sausage in" sort of thing. Anyway, despite him telling me to keep quiet, first thing I did when I got home was to tell me mum, "Gonna bring you a jelly home tomorrow" and she said, "Make it a strawberry one if you can, not one of those lime ones." Next day, I was travelling in on the bus with the boss and we were near the shop when we notices an enormous queue for the shop stretching down the road. 'Good God, look at that!" he said, "Someone's told them about the jellies!" It turned out mum had told everyone. I couldn't help blushing and gave myself away but I nearly got the sack for that.

It's always been Swad to me - never Swadlincote. It's the same with Woodville. I dunna call that Woodville, I call it 'Box' after John Knowles' Wooden Box Limited.

Before Swadlincote had a bus park the main picking up and dropping off was along side the Town Hall in Midland Road. This was a very convenient stop for visitors to the Market held on Friday and Saturday on the Delph and in the Town Hall. Harry Burnton also had a stall under the Shambles for many years from which he sold gents' outfitting. He also had access to the vaults under the Town Hall which he used as a fitting room and store. I was a customer of Harry's for many years as I used him to supply my school uniform as the official stockists in Burton were too expensive. The uniform was blue blazer with grey flannels. Harry provided grey jacket and brown trousers which was near enough! When I decided to buy a 'Teddy Boy' outfit I bought a suit from Harry and got him to modify it. He made a good job of it and it stood me in good stead until I developed more exotic tastes.

Along this side of the Town Hall was a lean-to building and at the top end of this was a kiosk belonging to Freddy Ellis. From this kiosk Freddy sold cigarettes and sweets through a hatch to the passing public. He also dispensed tea and light refreshments inside this establishment but such were the Lilliputian proportions of the building that it was full to overflowing with four customers. After more than four were to be accommodated then the overflow had to stand outside under the Shambles. Bus crews were good customers since they very often had time to nip in for a quick cuppa before proceeding on their journey refreshed by the drink and Freddy's wit and wisdom.

There were many public houses in Swadlincote when I was a boy, some of them remaining to this day. Walking from the bottom of Alexandra Road towards the main street you'd find The British Oak, The Bear, The Prince of Wales, The Nag's Head, Granville Arms, Market Inn, The Stanhope, Bull's Head and The Foresters. Half way up Coppice Side was the New Inn. Turning back and walking along Church Street we'd come to the Angel Inn which was near the church hence I supplied the name. A little further round at the back of the Park was the Railway Inn.

So Swadlincote was well served for drinking places. How they ever made a living, I will never know. To me as a small boy they were just places with frosted glass halfway up the windows, the smell of beer, tobacco smoke and loud men's voices. At the weekend there was sometimes a pianist so one heard singing, sometimes good but mostly bad and out of tune but who cares if one has had a few.

Swad people have always had a real distinctive sense of humour. They pull your leg if they can get it. They pull it especially when you bin somewhere and got into any trouble - if they can get owt on you, they pull your leg for all eternity.

If it grows, we sell it

I remember many of the shops in the High Street. One were Woolies where all the goods were sixpence or under at that time. If you bought a teapot you paid sixpence for the pot and threepence for the lid. Very close was Wilton's Bazaar and opposite was Dunn's Hat Shop, kept by two unmarried ladies, Mollie and Lorna. I sometimes went in there, for hats were fashionable then and gossiped with them. Further up on the opposite side were Ilsley's, the butchers, the candy store and the Maypole. Here, my best memory as a child was watching them slap butter into shape between two pieces of wood. I searched for the Maypole whilst mother was being served, but I never found it.

My favourite shop in Swadlincote was Bellfields because of all the toys. It was lovely. We used to look for all our Christmas presents in there and we'd press our noses against the window, dreaming of buying all the toys. I'd go in and look at the doll's house furniture. They had such a lovely selection and I remember my sister and I had a doll's house, one year. Oh, we loved it! It was beautiful, with this lovely little furniture. I'd love to know where it is now. Then there was the leather shop - Mr Wright's, next to the candy store. Mum and Dad took me down there and bought me a satchel when I passed my eleven plus and was going to the convent.

At the bottom of Swad's High Street was the posh shop - Miss Wright's. They sold really nice, good quality smart stuff, but it was a bit more pricey. If you were going to a wedding or something, my mum would go to Miss Wright's or Miss Buxton's at Gresley; it was one or the other.

I know of a woman who travelled all over the place to find a dress for a Twenty-Fifth Wedding Anniversary do, and she still had to come back to Swad to get something, because she hadn't got shoes or anything, but then she ended up at Miss Wright's shop and got just what she wanted in the first place. She says that she's still got the dress she bought. It was royal blue. It must be nearly twenty years old now. I wonder if she's kept it in moth balls. Miss Wright's shop was taken over by Claire Edmonds in 1977, when Miss Wright retired. Claire, a local person, kept up the tradition of good quality clothes until she too retired in 1998..

The A1 Candy Stores, in addition to sweets, also sold Lyons' ice-cream. Lyons' produced a hard ice-cream in the shape of a long cylinder encased in paper, an amount

I remember crowds of paper kids including myself, outside the Mail office in West Street waiting for the Mails to arrive in an old black taxi, Reuben Harris and his missus shouting 'Football Mail' and then we'd go to Ward's cake shop and tuck in to massive scones, full of soda.

was cut off depending on how much one paid, the paper removed and one portion stuck in a cornet. My favourite ice cream was Dythams, made in Woodville and it could be obtained from local shops or from their own 'Okey Carts,' both motorised and horsedrawn, which toured the district. I have never tasted better and it passed the acid test of being the only make my pet bull terrier would eat!

Apart from the pubs, you could meet folk for a drink in a lot of places. A few yards down the road on the opposite side of the road was the Arcadia Milk Bar where shoppers could slake their thirst. Should you require more substantial fare, a meal could be obtained at Topliss's Café in Midland Road, next door to the Council Office: I believe that they produced an impressive sandwich. Waterfields had a popular café behind their bread and cake shop in High Street. Traditional meat and two veg served by traditionally dressed waitresses in a room warmed by a traditional coal fire!

Its market place, the Delph
Stalless now, pedestrianised,
Hears the echoes of traders' cries,
And yearns for its former self.
For the flap of canvas
On the open stall
For the banter and yell
The shout and the bawl
For the jokes and the spiel
That got people to buy
For the sniffing nose
And staring eye
For the wait in the evening
When the bargains would start
On the market place
That was Swad's heart.

I always remember, in front of the Granville Arms, there used to be a man there, I think he came from Derby, Potters, and they sold rolls of lino and that. I can see him now, how he were there with his brown warehouse coat on and they'd roll a roll of lino out and slap it a bit, "an' who'll offer me this, for that?" Whether they were remnants or off cuts, I don't know, but they always had a roll of it, and they used to just lean it up agen the wall at the Granville Arms, and tie it with a piece of string. In them days there used to be this oil cloth, what you had on the kitchen table, which didn't need washing, you just used wipe it over and they would sell that too.

There were one feller he used to make toffee, and they used to call it Tommy Dodd, and he used to have a big notice up, "Tommy Dodd, made at Swad", and you'd see him with this hook, and they used get hot toffee and wrap it round this hook and then break it off when it set, and sell it in chunks of Tommy Dodd.

The centre piece in Swad was the market on the Delph. It was a meeting place and a bargaining place for people with only coppers in their pockets and purses. All the stall holders dispensed what goods they managed to sell with witty repartee which rarely changed from week to week but still managed to raise a laugh. One of the many characters that stand out in my mind was an old lady. She was actually probably no more than forty but in those days when a woman had lost a husband, she dressed in a long black dress with black button-up boots and very rarely married again. Many looked old before their time. The widow's pension was pitiful and this lady would carry a large straw bag in which she would put all the trimmings off cabbages that had been put in the bins at the side of the stalls. If there was a busted orange or apple, trodden underfoot, it would find its way into her bag and she would regularly approach Lenny Blankley with the two of them sticking to the following script, pretty much every week.

Lenny: Here again are you? How much money you got?

Lady: I got fourpence in my purse.

Lenny: Rabbits are sixpence so it's no good keep standing there, you won't get one.

Old lady moves a bit to one side so he can serve others but she doesn't move away from the stall.

Lenny: No good waiting. Rabbits are sixpence. I'm going for a pint.

He comes back from the pub and there she stands.

Lenny: Are you b... haunting me?

Lady shuffles her feet and looks down at the floor. Meanwhile, the ice in the fish boxes is starting to turn to water and this is when the patient market shoppers move in, saying things like, "Is this fish fresh? Dunna smell that fresh!"

Lenny: You had it for next to nowt last week!

The old lady still stands at the side of the stall looking sad.

Lenny: How much money did you say you had? Fourpence? Let's see it.

She rummages around and produces four pennies.

Lenny: Hold it upside down and shake it. I bet you've got a ten bob note sewed in your corsets.

The old lady, realising the Saturday night play is nearly over, looks visibly brighter.
Lenny reaches for the smallest rabbit off the hook and takes the fourpence. She tucks the rabbit in her bag and moves away and as she is going, Lenny says, "You're ruining me!" and gives her her fourpence back. You learnt a lot about compassion and humanity on that market.

One stall in particular fascinated me as a child - a man who sat with jars of worms on his table. Thinking about it now, he probably dug them up out of the garden. But anyway, he'd got them pickled in these jars. Then he used to deliver his lecture on worms that were parasites in the intestines of human beings all over the world.

When he had totally horrified everybody about all the places he said he had been to, and he'd drawn a crowd around him, he'd produce a cardboard box from under the table and trot out all this herb medicine in bottles.

Of course, not many people had got six pence to buy a bottle, but one or two people did because according to him it cured every ill known to humanity and as part of the entertainment of the market they occasionally believed him.

One Friday night, my family were all at the market and as all the stallholders were packing up, Dad was talking to Lenny, pulling his leg because Lenny had only one very large cod fish left on the stall. 'It's a pity you've got to take that fish back Lenny,' he said, 'It'll only go off and smell. Tell you what, I'll give you two bob for it and no more.' Dad kept arguing with him until Lenny got fed up with him and in the end, Lenny threw the fish at dad and said , 'Give us a tanner Charlie and clear off!'

 The Harrisons stood out from the market throng
And so did the fish man in a children's song.

The Harrison sisters really stood out. I think it was the fact that, there were four females, who ran a market stall. They were able to drive a truck, load a truck and unload a truck, put a market stall up and the rest of it. They were quite capable of doing anything that most people expect a man to be around to do, but the Harrison sisters were able to do that on their own.

When I worked for Bob Kenny at Kenny's Garage at Stanton, the Harrison sisters had an A type Bedford truck, a brown one, and we used to service this truck. Whoever took it back up to the Harrison sisters' house would invariably find they'd come back with a box of fruit, and it use to amaze me. If you went up there in summer, you'd get over the niceties of delivering it back and she'd say, "Come into the garage," and all this fruit was in there and it was full of wasps, but they never seemed to bother the Harrison women. They just walked through the things. Wasps used to crawl up their arms into their hair, and they'd never even bother, and we'd stand back and cringe, while they went to collect a box of fruit to take back for the other lads at the garage.

For many years, the Harrisons had a monopoly on many goods on the market but eventually Mr. Vyce opened a stall. His method of selling was to shout his wares and prices, something the Harrisons never did. He also gave away his goods in printed paper bags which were complete with his name and bore the legend, 'If it grows, we sell it!' He certainly livened up the market and his shouting became more strident towards the end of an afternoon, after repeated visits to the Granville.

Len Blankley's claim to fame was that he regularly went round delivering to houses as late as half ten, eleven o'clock on a Saturday night. By then he'd be out of his mind with ale. 'Course he went from one pub to another and just loaded up. There was a story as told about him, that he called at The Open Anchor, which is just down the road here, and there was railings round the field and while he was there, somebody untied old Len's horse, pushed the shafts through the railings and then fastened the horse in the other side. When Len came out, it made him scratch his head. "Well I know'd you were thin," he said, "but I don't know how you got through there?" Of course he'd go to the pub and he'd fill a bottle up, which he'd keep under a bag on his cart and he supped it as he went along.

Lenny's brother told me that when they lived in Woodville, then, he said, it would be a regular thing for me dad to go down the yard, on a Sunday morning, a real cold, frosty morning, he says, with haw frost hanging from the hedges, and there would be our Len, fast asleep on the cart, with haw frost hanging off his ears, and his poor old horse still in his shafts and as much as me dad grumbled at him, he said, you couldn't alter him.

They were a highly respected family really. When I were a boy, I remember that they would say that the Blankley's are going out this afternoon. Well, that meant that Mr Blankley was going out in his coach and four, with Mrs Blankley, and she used to have one of these here Gainsborough hats on. When they were going out on a Sunday afternoon ride we used to run up to the Toll Gate, Woodville, and watch 'em go. But I'm afraid old Lenny sort of let the side down, because he was what would be known as 'the black sheep' of the family, and his being drunk in charge of a horse, led him into court a lot, and on his hundredth conviction, they had a banner headline, in the *Mail*, saying, "Lennard hits a century," which meant, he'd made hundred appearances in court.

'Harrisons sold oranges - ten for two pence straight out of boxes on the lorry.'

But of course, it was something as he couldn't hide, and the local police knew him and they'd only got to sort of wait on the A50 till eleven o'clock time, and Len would come along there with the old horse taking him back 'ome. Probably fast asleep.

In West Street, behind Lush's Wet Fish Shop and up an alley beside the Empire Cinema was the entrance to Lush's Fish and Chip Restaurant. This was a popular venue with shoppers and cinema goers. One could round off a night's entertainment with a substantial meal for about a florin (10p). The tables had cloths on them, no plastic in those days, and the customer collected his order at the counter and took it to his table.

You could come straight out of the Empire, straight up the alley into Lush's, and you could either sit in the restaurant, if you were wealthy or you could go up the yard and stand in the queue and get your fish and chips from there. The thing I can remember about Lush's is the iron frame door with four panes of glass in it, and their Alsatian sat outside. It wasn't a very nice walk up there if you wasn't used to it, because the Alsatian used sit on the yard and just wander about.

The sight of Rex the Alsation was enough to make you think of going home and forgettin' all about your chips but the proprietor when I was a lad was a chap called Bob Clamp and he used to growl at Rex, more than Rex used to growl at him. He certainly knew how to keep the dog quiet, so we could enjoy queueing for the chips and they really were great chips. A shillings worth in them days would feed a small army.

The other side of the serving hatch was like a restaurant, and nothing plush, but someone'd shout through, "I see you're rich tonight." You'd be sitting in there with your cup of tea and your fish and chips, and bread and butter.

Me mam tells me that I was born at a quarter to five in the morning and whilst she was in labour, she was frying fish. In them days there was no restriction on how long you stayed open you see. Strangely enough, I don't know whether that's got anything to do with it but I hate fish, I can't eat it. I've tried and tried but I cannot eat fish. Neither fresh, nor tinned, nor nothin'. I've been frying for others though for many years when I worked at Lush's. My sister, she never served. She had a three pan stove. The middle pan was always fish and the two end pans were chips. It was my job, together with Lena, my sister-in-law, to keep an eye on the chips and to fetch them out when they were cooked.

We used to open then on a Friday, Saturday and Monday. We only had a certain allocation of fat which was peanut oil and when that was gone, we had to close. This

We used to stand outside the chip shop 'til they'd got some batter bits and then they used call us in and give us a bag of batter bits. Delicious.

was the end of the war and people were desperate for food and one thing and another. They used to be queuing out of that fish shop at ten past nine in the morning and we always reckoned to close from one o' clock to quarter past two for dinner. And we'd shut the door at about half past twelve and we'd get the queue cleared by two o'clock. We grabbed what we could eat and we'd be open again at quarter past two. Very often, we'd be closed at four o' clock because we'd used up our allocation of fat.

I first started using the Nag's Head when I was demobbed from the Army in 1958. The building was in a prominent position and was sturdily built. It had four public rooms on the ground floor, ie a large bar that covered much of the frontage area of the pub, a snug and two lounges.

The bar occupied two thirds of main bar area and access was gained from High Street. Behind the bar was a glass case which contained the England football caps won by Mrs Hall's first husband, Ben Warren. Ben was born in Newhall and played eight years for Derby County, his career lasting from 1899 to 1911.

At weekends the pub was packed to capacity especially on nights when big dance bands attended the nearby dance hall, The Rink. The beer was always in tip top condition and was arguably the best drink in the town. Mrs Hall, a charming lady, was always insistent on a clean glass for every drink you ordered.

When I was courting my wife Janet, we would call in there and the atmosphere was always friendly. Everyone was made welcome. When the top local amateur boxing hero of that time, Jack Bodell, was on TV, the men would be invited into the kitchen to supply tea or coffee (free of charge) for the ladies. The two lounges were on the West Street end of the building, a large club room upstairs was very popular and was used for wedding receptions and parties. It was a sad night when the pub closed its door for the final time. Many people will never understand why arguably the best pub in the town was demolished.

John Avery's dad and mother kept the local pub, The Bear. When Mr and Mrs Avery came behind the bar, you knew instantly who the landlord and landlady were. They would be dressed up as if they were going to a big dance or something. But you know - they were really mine host and hostess. And a lot of stars went there. Ah, namely, what were his name? As used to, 'Shut that door', Larry Grayson. Old Larry often used call in.

Larry used to sell things out of a case on Swad market, mainly ties. And if he had a bad day, which he probably would do if the weather was bad - he'd hardly make anything. When he'd paid his pitch rental, he wouldn't have much left. If he'd had a bad day, he'd always say he could rely on the kindness of Bill Avery and get a bowl of soup or something. He said, "You know, for little or nothing," he said, "and I shall always respect him, to this day." On the day of Bill's funeral, Larry Grayson sent a beautiful spray of roses and he attended the funeral himself, of course. The Avery's always seemed to be up with that sort of people. They had miners in there as well as anybody else, but they always seemed to get on well with the people in entertainment and that.

In 1948, I'd go to school on the bus, travelling from Newhall to Burton. At that time the 'Midland Red,' or to give it its full title 'The Birmingham and Midland Motor Omnibus Company' had almost a monopoly on local bus services.

Competition to provide public transport services had been fierce during the 1920's and the first casualty had been the 'Burton-Ashby Light Railway'. This was a tramway system which linked the railway station of Burton, Ashby and Castle Gresley plus all the villages en route. It had opened in 1906, being initially successful, but had declined against the competition of the more flexible bus system. The last tram rattled and clanged into the Swadlincote sheds on February 19th, 1927, which left the numerous local bus companies to 'fight' for the most lucrative routes.

Incidentally, the tram sheds are still in existence. They are now being used as a small industrial park and are situated next to Eureka Park. A few tram poles which held up the power lines are still in being and also inspection covers in pavements along the routes with the company name on them. Although trams were common in towns, it was unusual to have them in rural areas.

In addition to the local bus companies vying for routes, there was the large 'Midland Red' organisation. They started taking over the local competition, in particular Parker's and also the Regent Bus Company, and built their garage in Swadlincote in 1931. This was symbolically erected in front of the defunct tram shed just off the Blue Bridge. The Golden Age of the railway was also coming to an end.

The death knell of the railway in Swadlincote sounded in 1964 when the station closed and the lines were taken up. One of the platforms is still to be seen behind the Fire Station. When I was very young, I was fascinated by steam trains and I liked to watch operations from the Blue Bridge. When I saw an engine approaching I used to peer over the wall waiting for it to appear from under it. A large cloud of black smoke and smuts usually preceded it and I was enveloped in this. I returned home smelling of smoke with the blackest face imaginable.

Travelling to work every day was one way in which friendships were struck up. Passengers tended to catch the same bus each day and so a vaguely 'club' spirit prevailed. If a regular passenger was absent one morning it was noted by the 'regulars' who would speculate as to his or her absence and express concern. Quite a few marriages were initiated by the 'friendly Midland Red!'

Another example of social change which speaks volumes of how times have changed was that on certain buses general passengers did not sit on the back six rows of seats as these were used by miners returning home in their 'pit black' having finished a shift. No cars and no pithead baths!

During the war a bus powered by gas was experimented with. The gas was carried in a cylinder which had the appearance of a dustbin on wheels and attached to a tow bar at the rear of the bus. I understand that its performance left something to be desired.

We were only served by single decker buses until after the war. Double decker buses were introduced soon after and I remember my mother, on seeing the first one, vowing not to travel on one as it would tip up going round the traffic island in Midland Road!.

Who was the driver who surreptitiously donned a long wig and caused consternation amongst the passengers? Why? They thought a *woman* was driving. Gasp! Happy Days indeed!

I joined the 'friendly Midland Red' in the late 50s. It was winter, and I was a bricklayer at the time, and as so often happens in bad weather, brickies are laid off because of the frosts.

We usually found other work to keep us going until the weather improved, that's why I went to the Midland Red for a job driving.

I was used to driving lorries, but I'd never driven a bus, so before I was accepted as a bus driver I had to go on a ten day course at Birmingham for a PSV licence.

The instructor, an ex-army bloke, stood in the gangway of a decker and said, "Who's driven a crash box?" and one man name Rattle replied, "I've driven every sort of vehicle there is."

"Right," said the instructor, "Now who's going first in the sweat box?" I wanted to get my turn over with so I went first.

I drove down Hagley Road, and through the centre of Birmingham, and when I'd

'When it came dark on the market, they used have hurrican' lamps, hangin' an' swingin' in the breeze.'

finished, the instructor said, "You've driven well."

Then a Scotsman who'd driven on the Glasgow Corporation went second. He was all right until he came to turn at the public toilets, in New Street, and for the life of him he couldn't get round the corner. The instructor had to stop the traffic, and back the decker up, so the Scotsman could make another attempt.

Rattle, the man who said he'd driven everything there is, played a tune on the gear box, and the instructor said to him "Rattle by name and Rattle by nature!"

I went on to Leicester from there for the Commissioners' Test, on the Highway Code. The only problem I thought I might have was with the colour blind test, but they asked me questions on the colours of flowers in a basket from a picture on the wall. Now, we all know that roses are often red, daffodils yellow, leaves green, and a basket is either light brown or dark brown.

It was common sense that got me through, but I did tell the examiner afterwards that I had some degree of colour blindness.

"Well," he said. "You know the sequence of the lights, don't you?"

"Yes, of course," I replied.

"Then you'll have no trouble," he said, and he was right.

When I'd completed all the questions, I travelled back to Birmingham to be fitted out with a uniform. It was black, edged with red, and peak cap. A heavyweight material for winter, plus overcoat, and a light weight uniform for the summer months.

I then spent a day or so route learning at the Swadlincote Depot. The buses were dependable, and had clippies when I first joined the team. Later, one-man operated buses took over some of the routes. The Inspectors were always on top form; we had to run on time, they made sure of that, and we had safe driving awards.

The Midland Red had a motto - *We never stop running* - but the fog was a real problem sometimes. We don't seem to get the pea soupers that we had in the late '50s and '60s.

Anyway, I remember one night, we were doing the Gresley run, coming from Linton. We were on lates, and the fog was really thick. Inspector or no Inspector, it was impossible to keep on time. The clippies were having to lean out of the door, to see where we were going, and in places where visibility was nil they had to walk in front of the bus as a guide. When my clippie rang the bell three times for emergency stop and said, "Do you know where you are?" I wiped the window inside for the umpteenth time, and said, "No."

Back came the reply, "Well, you've just driven down Common Side." I knew then that it was time to pack it in. Common Side wasn't even on my route. So we had to get back on track, then limp slowly back to the bus station, park up, and wait for the fog to lift before we could finish the shift.

The garage had both football and cricket teams, also a representative Company cricket team. Drivers, conductors, and garage staff were picked from all the garages in the Midlands for that.

I was one of the fortunate ones to be picked for the representative team, and to me that was one of the perks of the job. We had great days out, and we had our fair share of wins, which wasn't surprising since we had a good team of players.

For a long time, the Midland Red, like Salt's shop, represented stability in the area, but then the winds of change began to blow.

My memories of Swadlincote start with shopping trips from the village where I lived, at the end of a bus route. On the hour, every hour, the single decker bus would deposit its passengers and conductor opposite the shop, the driver would drive the bus almost to the Chapel, then reverse in front of the shop with the conductor waving his arms importantly while standing in the middle of the road. As children we thought how brave he was standing there in the road whilst the bus got closer and closer.

In those days the driver would often stop the bus directly outside a passenger's home. I have seen the conductor help a young mother off the bus with her shopping, children and pushchair, he even put the pushchair ready for the youngest child. On another occasion a conductress carried the shopping of an elderly lady to her door. The lady had fallen in Salt's shop so someone from Salts had accompanied her to the bus station, waited with her until her bus had arrived, the shop assistant told the bus crew what had happened and saw her to her door, then asked a neighbour to keep an eye on her until her son arrived home from work.

Turn from the Delph to the High Street
And here and there you'll see
Vestiges, mementoes
Of what Swad used to be.
The collieries that fuelled the town
Now decorate a plate
To hang upon the fireplace
Over the empty grate.
Go inside and buy one
And underneath your feet
A treasure; tiled in black and white
A Roman mosaic with neat
Copperplate letters sloping across
The doorway that once took you into Salt Bros.

All the trimmings - Salt's

Mention Salt's and people say
They can remember to this very day
Contraptions and devices that whizzed round the store
Through every department from floor to floor.
A wooden ball on rails
A catapulted casket
A torpedo sucked into a tube
To a child's eyes, all fantastic
Ways of sending money
From counter to cashier.
The mechanisms hummed, white hot
On sale days, twice a year
When people swarmed to Swad to spend
Their windfall co-op dividend.

Fifty odd years ago the three shops in Swadlincote belonging to Salt Brothers, were well known, not only for the fact that they sold just about everything, but also because it was done with the utmost efficiency and politeness.

There was no 'help yourself and pay at the check out' then, it was a case of asking the assistant standing behind the counter to serve you and you could guarantee that he or she would do their best to help you find just what you wanted.

The haberdashery shop in Swadlincote's High Street was my favourite. Upstairs, on the right, you could find ladies' underwear and nightclothes, and on the left, overlooking the High Street, you could have a good laugh at yourself through the conveniently placed mirror, whilst trying on the hats, and wishing at the same time that you could squeeze into a smaller size of that coat you fancied to go with the hat. Then of course, while the Second World War still raged, you would need clothing coupons to buy them, for most things were rationed.

Downstairs, the shelves were well stocked with bed linen, tablecloths, cushion covers and towels, in fact everything a household needs. At the rear end of the shop was a large range of materials. Of course, Salt's had all the trimmings that went with the materials, which helped: buttons, belts, lace, sequins, and best of all - the dress patterns only cost one shilling and sixpence, that's the equivalent of 7$\frac{1}{2}$p in the '90s.

My Grandma Parry had been a seamstress before she died, and my dad inherited her Singer treadle sewing machine. When I was thirteen in 1943, she taught me how to use it and I soon found that I had an aptitude for sewing. I must have inherited her love of making things also, because after seeing the materials in Salt's, I was hooked and over the years that followed I learned how to make anything from a simple apron, to a dress and coat ensemble.

The materials were different from today. Cotton was cotton, it wasn't mixed with anything man made, and the same thing applied to silk, satin and lace. There was little problem with static in clothes. Colours though were not as bright as they are today in the '90s. That would not have been appropriate through the war years anyway.

The shop opposite Woolworths belonged to Salt Brothers, and was known as the Hardware Department. Upstairs, you would find bedroom furniture, tables and chairs and downstairs carpets, kitchen ware and garden equipment. Further up the High Street was the third shop belonging to Salt Brothers known as the Men's Department. This was also well stocked with gents' shoes on the right, and on the left - men's underwear, suits and coats, etc.

A lot of the things, certainly in the crockery line, were from the local industries, like Green's potteries and much of the earthenware was made locally. They also catered for the fact that a lot of the workmen bought their boots from there for jobs in the local industries. Miners boots certainly had to be made to a specific safety level, determined by the national Coal Board and they'd buy their moleskin trousers from Salt's too.

Paying for goods at Salt's was quite an experience especially for the children accompanying their parents on a day out shopping. Often the little ones would stand there with their mouths open, looking at the wires overhead, and wondering what they were for, just as I did when I was small.

The cash and invoice for the goods were placed in a small cylinder with a screw bottom, which was then attached to a wire overhead, and at the operation of a lever, it was sent speeding on its way, to a central cash desk. The cylinder containing the change and invoice stamped - 'Paid with thanks', was then returned in the same way to the assistant at the counter; all very quick and efficient. It was known as the Lamson and Paragon catapult. Later, through the years, the wires were removed and replaced by a

Which are the two funniest shops in Swad?
Salt's and Boots - because Salt's sell boots and Boots sell salts.

metal shute which operated on compressed air, this sent the small cylinder on its way with a great whoosh!

Everyone was fascinated by the Lamson and Paragon catapult. It was my job to switch the compressor on every day, and I was surprised just how many people wanted to have a go with it, grown ups as well as children. That method of payment would be too slow for the people of today though, because it sometimes took nearly ten minutes for a transaction to be made, but nobody ever complained. The chute made a special noise as it sped the cylinder on its way to the central control; everyone remembers it.

We sometimes played tricks on each other, and me and another girl behind the counter had a bit of a laugh one day. I put a spider in one of the cylinders and sent it on to Jane at the cash desk, then we stood back and waited for the scream when she opened it.

When we used to sing on the 'Sermons' at Chapel, me mum used take us to Salt's and fit us out. Which she'd already paid for on a Salt's cheque. You paid a shilling a week, for twelve weeks and you had a twelve shilling cheque to go and spend then. And I know there used to be perhaps two or three families used give their money to me mother. And they would draw out that, they got a cheque on the third week, after they'd only paid three shilling sort of thing. But of course, they had to carry on paying for the next nine weeks. And me mum always used to say, "Well I want to save mine for when it's 'sermons' so I can fit the lads out." There were three of us. We used go there and old Ezzie Salt, as was the head man then, he'd come along there and he'd see you being sat on the counter, having your sandals tried on and that, as you was getting rigged out.

We'd got a football team in Swadlincote called Swadlincote Amateurs. We used to play in the Derby District Wednesday League and we asked Mr Ezzie Salt about a set of shirts for the team. Could he get us a set? And he agreed. So we had all sorts of things like Beetle drives, whist drives, anything to get money to pay for them. We went to Mr Salt to pay him and he got the bill, signed it, 'Paid with thanks' and then he surprised us by giving us the money back to start the club off. He paid for the shirts himself. I should think he must be one of the first sponsors of football shirts in the country!

I can remember having to buy one of the famous Green's yellow mixing bowls at Salt's. It was a busy Friday afternoon. Accompanying me was my six year old son David in his pram and trotting alongside on his lead was our waif and stray dog, whom we'd named Sunday on account of him being found a few weeks earlier on a Sunday in Castle Gresley. The pram was parked close to the store doorway, the dog fastened by his lead to the pram - you could do things like that in those days - and after buying the mixing bowl, I made my way to the doorway. A crowd of shoppers were blocking my way. A real air of panic was building, and then a voice cried, "The dog won't let us out and there's people who can't get in!" "Let me out then we can all get out!" I shouted. "You can't!" shouted this irate woman who was clutching a large bow to her bosom and a general scuffle ensued with Sunday barking and the ladies in the shop all jostling each other. "I own the dog!" I cried, as the crowd parted allowing me to sally forth clutching my precious bowl and then locating pram, child and dog and hurrying away. Such panic contrasted with the usual calm and sedate atmosphere of the Salt's shops.

Salt's sales were celebrated affairs. I remember my first sale. Staff warned me, "Stay clear when you open the doors at 9.00am, people go mad for their bargains!"

Standing behind the door with the crowd on the other side, I opened the door. This man grabbed me, pulled me into the display window, chucked me on a bed, with him falling on top of me and said, "Stick a 'sold' ticket on that!" He got his bargain, a bed at half price.

Another funny incident was when I was transferred through to the kitchen department, where you could buy kitchen cabinets and sink units. I had to wash all the sinks down. None of them were connected to anything but I forgot that and when I got to the last one, out of force of habit, I emptied my bucket with hot soapy water down one of the sinks and it flooded the whole shop floor.

I can remember my first interview for the job. It took place in a little dark room and it was Mr R. Salt interviewed me. Some days later, Mum and Dad were told that I'd got a job along with my sister. She took me to meet Mr Fairbrother and he showed us around. I was terrified. I started on a Tuesday and had a half day off. It must have been a holiday time. I joined the club when I was older and I bought my clothes with it after saving for twenty weeks and getting my bonus. I remember buying my wedding shoes and some of my wedding outfit with cards I'd saved up. My starting wage was £2. 10s. 4d. And I gave my parents £2 of that. I loved my days at Salt's and stayed for nearly ten years. All the staff were respectful and the customer was 'always right' (whether they

were or not.) After I left, I still went back to the shop to get things for my baby. What I miss most about Salt's is the companionship of the staff - the fun and laughter we shared and the committment to 'serve'.

I survived only one day at Salt's. I went there for a job before I went to Ensors. Me mother took me down because we were pretty good customers at Salt's with four lads and she took me down. She got talking to Ezzie Salt and asked him if he could find me a job and he agreed to let me start the following week. On the morning, I turned up for work.

"Right," he says, "Go up to the warehouse and see Mr So-and-So and he'll load the handcart up for you."

So, I went up to the warehouse and saw them loading this handcart up. Buckets and lino and stuff and all sorts of pots and pans. They wanted it all delivering. I'd never been out of the district and I'd got to go as far as Stanton with this handcart. Well, I set off and I got as far as the bridge going by Swad Park and it was that heavy I couldn't push it over the top of the bridge.

A chap happened to be passing by and he said, "My God, they've loaded you up 'aven't they my lad!" I said, "They have and I can't push it. I've got no end of heavy lino and stuff on and carpets and things and dolly tubs."

Anyway, he gave me a push up with it over this hill and I managed to start going across the level and I'd gone another half mile when I just panicked. I didn't know the road to Stanton, so I left the handcart there and went running home. I think we were molly-coddled a bit too much really. Me mother asked me what the matter was and I told her what had happened. She took me back to see Ezzie Salt and he tried to mek all sorts of excuses and that , saying, "Well, I'll see what I can do about that, whether we can take some of the stuff off then" and I said to me mum, "No, I'm not stopping here" and that were my day at Salt's. Never went back again.

We used to deliver goods by van and we also had a horse and dray and we'd use bikes and handcarts too. We would deliver anything we sold free of charge. In fact, if you ordered a broom stail, we would deliver this as far as Packington once a week and local twice a week. One elderly lady rang up from top Midway for two light bulbs and said, "While you're bringing them, go along to Colliers and get me half a pound of liver, put it in to the parcel and I'll pay the driver." You see that was what we called personal

The one thing about Salt's was, they never displayed female underwear in the windows. It wasn't considered quite the thing to do. But at harvest time, Chapel Anniversary times, they would often have a good display of outfits for the ladies. Women would be buying a new outfit, especially for the day - Methodists went in more for the Sunday School Anniversaries and Salt's catered for it all. Very flowery hats, that were like a garden.

service! We also once fitted curtains to an inside wall as the man said it was cold to his back when he was sitting in front of the fire.

From the clothing department, we would go out to people's house and measure for a suit, jacket or trousers. This was for anyone working shifts, ill or disabled. Suits would take about two weeks and most of these were made for us by a tailoring company in Nottingham. We had a very good range. If some trousers you had were too long, we had them shortened for you, ready for the next day for a shilling. One lady I remember, just up Hill Street, said she'd bought these grey flannel trousers for her son to play cricket in. He fell on one knee and got all grass stains on them. So she washed this one leg and it ran up an inch and she then needed the other leg shortened to match. We did oblige but it was a shilling.

I think I must have been thick at the time but in hindsight it's funny to remember that whenever a lady came into the shop for jodhpurs, the manager always said, "I'll measure these" and he had to take them upstairs. I never got to measure any of these ladies for jodhpurs. It must have been a speciality job!

A local vicar once came in and I served him. He just wanted a pair of flannel trousers to change into in the evenings. He chose a pair and said, 'How much are these?' I said, "4/11 1/2" He said, "Goodness, I'll take two pairs, another wedding and it'll pay for these!" I won't say which church he came from!

Having served in the Royal Navy until demobbed in 1946, I returned to Salt Bros in the clothing department under the manager, Mr. Albutt. My wage then was £4 per week. Men and senior ladies got paid every week and girls got paid every month as the wage was too small to put up each week, but that didn't stop them applying. There was often a twelve month waiting list. Out of each week's money, we had to give 2p to Burton Hospital and the Red Cross.

Most of the staff who worked there were very loyal and started work before time and stayed after time. There was no union. You didn't just have to do one job and of course, there were no calculators. If you didn't know what five tenths of a shilling was, the manager would soon have you on your toes. Despite having the lowest wage of any trade, the staff were very happy and I didn't know what the word 'bored' meant until I was over twenty.

The standards in the shops were extremely high. For example, we didn't have cleaners at Salt's. All of it was done by the staff - clean windows inside and out, clean floors,

It was always busy, and I know when Salt's was going to close, I think people wondered what on earth they were going to do without it, and my next door neighbour - well, she wasn't my next door neighbour at the time - she always had her knickers from there. It was the only word you could call them - knickers (you couldn't call them anything else) and she bought lots and lots of pairs of these knickers, 'cause she didn't want to face life without any of Salt's underwear. I happened to do a bit of ironing for her the other day, and I think the knickers are just beginning to wear out, but what she'll do then I don't know, but she is well into her seventies, so she might just manage.

toilets, the works. I remember cleaning all the windows on six 'steps' from Hunters down to Melias (which is now Birds) and to Gardeners. The manager would supervise and say, "Have you nearly finished, John?" - even though my name was Arthur. It didn't really matter though. I think they called everybody John 'cause I suppose with the amount of staff they had, it would be a job to remember. He'd come out and say, "Ah, you've missed two bits up there, John. You'd best do them again." They would be the size of postage stamps and I'd have to do the whole lot again - all the clean ones as well.

I married a girl from the shop and Mr. Salt came to me and he said, "You're married now, John, aren't you?" and I thought, 'Well, me name's Arthur and I've bin here all these years you see'. But I just said, 'Yes, sir.' And he said, "Well, there's some money for you in your packet, a rise." I got it late on Saturday night, half past six. You never got it on Friday, so you couldn't spend it. Anyhow, I gave my wife the packet and when she opened it there were five shillings in it, which would be twenty-five pence. Twenty-five pence to keep the wife on!

My job was in the Drapery department. We sold curtains and towels. Charles Fairbrother was the manager then and John King was his second in command. My first wage packet was £24 but it went up quite a bit before I left.

The customers often expected us to know things, like, for instance: one woman come in to buy some curtain material, and she looked at me and said, "How much material do I need for a wide window?"

She hadn't bothered to measure it, because she thought that whoever served her would know how wide it was.

Another lady came in one day, and asked for some net curtains to put on her front door. "What size would you like, madam," I said, and she reached for her handbag and showed me a photograph of her front door.

"Oh yes, you need nets about three inches long, madam" I said, smiling at her. She laughed and I was glad she could see the funny side.

It was a good job working at Salt's, and I probably wouldn't have gone elsewhere if they hadn't closed. First they shut the Men's Clothing department and then later announced that they were shutting the Drapery department as well, so by then everyone got the message. It must have been really hard for those who had worked there for many years. When I left, I went to Wraggs and Woodwards and worked on a press. I've still kept one of Salt's orange carrier bags that they used to use, as a memento of my time there.

To the locals it was unthinkable that Salt's would ever close, until the rumour began to go round, and then when it finally did close its doors for the last time in 1982, after a century of trading, everyone felt stunned and kept saying - "What are we going to do without Salt's?" It was indeed a great loss. Change is very unsettling and Salt's represented stability and all the old values. However, time moves on, and we have to move with it.

So Salt's doors closed and in the mines
The cages all slammed shut.
Ski slopes covered clay holes
And the scorching kilns and the soot
And in the morning and evening hooters
Were distant reminders of when
A sulphurous blanket fogged the town
Salt fired choking and grey. Then
Swad's wealth was underground, yellow and black
And it only came to light if you bent your back
To dig it out whether coal or clay
Pits, pots and pipes and roll on pay day.

chapter three

Pits, Pots & Pipes

Not all black and white

Seeing Swad
it was difficult for people nowadays
younger than me
to figure this out
but Swad wasn't in colour in those days
it was in
black and white
especially at that time
of the evening
it was smoke
I mean
this would be before the days of smokeless fuel
you got all the industry in Swad
and
it was like
going down into a well
like
going down into the depths of hell
but it was great.

The industrialistion of the area began with the Industrial Revolution and the tremendous demand for coal. It was in the early 19th Century that the first deep mines were sunk to increase production to fulfil this demand.

In the middle of the 19th Century, politicians and social workers became concerned about public health and the lack of sanitation. Various bills were passed in Parliament and the upshot was an explosion in the demand for all forms of sanitary work (WC, Bowls, Sinks, Urinals, etc) and, more importantly, drain pipes. The clay around Swadlincote was ideally suited to the salt-glazing process and only occurred in about half-a-dozen other areas in Britain. The call for sewer pipes was phenomenal and it is claimed that at one time 70% of the total production of salt glazed pipes in the UK was in South Derbyshire.

The down side of the rapid industrialisation was the devastation of the landscape. Great spoil heaps appeared at collieries and huge scars were formed by the 'open-hole' production of clay. Chimneys and kilns proliferated, all spewing out smoke and unpleasant fumes. The area eventually resembled a lunar landscape with a touch of Hades. Rene Cutforth, the eminent local-born journalist and writer, said in his autobiogragphy that "Swadlincote was so ugly it made you laugh."

It is remarkable that in my lifetime, almost all this has disappeared. It developed quickly and it died just as quickly. All over a timespan of two centuries.

Obviously, there's a magic about a place, I suppose when you're a five, six year old. But it's when you get older you start to realise that the area immediately around Swad, and parts of Swadlincote in fact were rubbish tips. As you come into Swad, what they call Coppice side, was all clay holes, and Wraggs and Woodwards were at the bottom. They would be belching smoke from the kilns, and there'd be all the rattle and bang of trucks and tubs being moved round.

When it was raining, you had a uniform grey colour everywhere, and believe me it *was* uniform grey.

Down against Midland Road we had the railway coming through. The other side of Midland Road was a colliery called 'Old Shoddy' and there was Holt's pottery which was right next to it just at the bottom on Midland Road.

There were dozens and dozens of small pipe works and potteries in the back streets of Swadlincote and Church Gresley. There was Holts and Robinsons at the bottom of Alexander Hill, where the Majestic Cinema was, now Kwik Save.

There was Hawfield's brick works that was just across the other side of Swadlincote. There was Nadins Pit Swadlincote, just along Hearthcote Road, I mean, starting in Church Gresley, just coming into Swadlincote. There was the colliery at the top of the hill, which was always dusty and grimy. You couldn't even see Church Gresley properly until the whole lot disappeared. They had to put up with subsidence as well.

There was Mansfields just down a hollow, what they called Ducks in the hole, which is a funny old name, and TG Greens of course and Mason Cash. There were all the potteries round Swadlincote, and Swadlincote's in a hollow itself, and I suppose all the dust and rubbish would collect down there. So, when you look at it, it was a right grimy place I suppose, but as a kid you never saw that.

You could get a warm from it, round them kilns, when it was cold weather. Me and Audrey Burton used to go down the Albion for to tek the dinners. We used have to go by all these kilns. We used be frightened to death to go by there cause the men used be there, chucking coal and that in, and it'd flare out at ye.

On the left at the top of Hill Street, was a great yawning chasm, which I thought of as a black hole, and I had no idea what was in it. I didn't know it belonged to Wraggs and Woodwards, but the fear of the unknown in that hole, affected me every time I travelled to Swad. Swadlincote has always been linked with Hartshorne because it is the nearest town, but although fifty odd years ago, it was an effort to get there from Repton Road, we all looked forward to the trip on either the Trent bus which came from Derby every hour, or the Barton's bus, which came from Nottingham every two hours. The bus fare was only about 3d, hardly anything in today's money.

The journey took twenty minutes to get to Swad, and as the bus travelled along, I always got more and more fearful, knowing that the last hill into Swadlincote was very steep.

I had frightening visions of the wind blowing the bus into the hole, with me and everybody else in it, or if we managed to get down to the bottom of the hill, I wondered if the brakes were strong enough to hold the bus from careering into the shops at the bottom. This fear was with me from a small child until I was at least fifteen in 1949.

When Wraggs and Woodward's clay yard closed, I watched with great pleasure as the hole was filled in, and the blackness turned green as it was eventually carpeted with grass, and lined with trees. I heaved a sigh of relief every time I saw it, remembering my previous fears. Then one day, along came Tony Freeman and had it all dug up again.

Tony visualised a Dry Ski Slope Centre there, and with the help of Mark Butler and others, the idea was turned into reality. Whoever thought that Swadlincote would have such a futuristic facility. It certainly put Swadlincote once more on the map.

Our Pauline when she was little, she'd be two or three, she always suffered with what we thought was asthma but it wasn't. The doctor said it was the air, and it was like - well, it was salty, somehow, and he used say, "Get her away to the seaside." We used to tek her to the seaside every year for a week's holiday, and she used to lose it. It was kind of bronchial. I can't remember now what she called it, but anyway, later on in years, she suffered from hay fever. I worked in Salt's, and all the aluminium, all the saucepans, the kettles, we had to clean them every week, because the salt, the air, it like dulled them, you know what I mean.

My wife lived in the first house in Coppice Side, and their curtains just used to rot away. The salt smoke and that, used to rot the curtains and the windows; no matter how you cleaned them they would seem to have a blue sheen in the wind, in the glass. As if, you know, it was faulty glass or it hadn't been cleaned properly. But it was just the fact that they were salting. I know one bloke who used do it, old Sammy Collier. They always used make a joke about it, in the pub, they'd say, 'ay up 'ere's Sammy Collier's fog coming down!" 'Course he were head fireman at Woodwards, I think, as it was Wraggs and Woodwards. 'Course then the kilns sort of came on to the High Street, they were, what, within five yards of the High Street. So it were fairly obvious they were going to get it, and I mean, Swad used be thick with smoke, an acrid, sulphur type of smoke. Didn't do your health much good.

There were hooters for knocking off at lunch and everything. All the pipe works, and all the collieries surrounding the area had hooters, and these hooters was for starting time, knocking off and everything. Our hooter at Ensors stood out quite some way above the others, because it was off a ship, and it was a big powerful one that was, and everybody knew when Ensors went.

But the others - they'd all got different sounds, and we got so accustomed to them right from when we were kiddies, we could tell all the different sounds and what yard it was blowing from, and we used to say, "There you are look yer, that's Woodwards and that's the Albion, and that's Gresley Pit." You could tell the difference, they'd just got that little bit of difference in the sound.

If somebody got killed on the day shift, all the buzzers'd sound and the pit'd close down. At the time there were as many as ten or eleven collieries around here - Cadley Hill, Stanton Lane, Boardmans, Gresley, Donisthorpe, Rawdon, Measham, Granville, and Marquis among them. So you knew when a buzzer went at an unusual time, somebody had met a sad end. The women would all rally round and go and support the widow and it was nothing for the widow to be left with three or four children.

There is sometimes a feeling put across, that Swad has been a place of heavy tasks but menial tasks but I think if you look at it, there were some marvellous artists round here that were brought up from ordinary families from ordinary terraced houses in the back streets and avenues, who could produce beautiful designs and pottery. Bretby Art, Rowleys and Holts pottery is very sought after and holds a good price. It's the same with the mines. If you're going to dig a mine, you have to have all the machinery, and the necessary know how - how to put a passage through, where to tek your coal from, where your stone's going to be, where your water's going to be, how you're going to get rid of it. You need the pumps. You need all this engineering and some clever engineers to sort that out. You're going to need people who've been brought up in it, who've seen one phase of it develop, and then the next lot, see the other phase, see the way of teking it forward.

In a lot of ways, I don't think many of them have been praised enough, and they haven't been made to realise or they don't realise themselves just how clever they were.

I think Swad humour is very close to the Irish. It's a humour I love - a humour where you can throw insults at each other and not really tek any of it in. I remember a story when the ski slope first opened, that a group of people were waiting to go into the employment exchange. They'd obviously been out of work for sometime and another local walks by and shouts, "You don't want to go in there this morning. They're giving jobs away!" and somebody shouts back, "What sort of jobs?" and he says, "Stretcher bearers up the ski slopes!" It's the back handed humour. There was another incident where one chap was trying to describe another gentleman to his friend and he came out with a real piece of South Derbyshire when he said, "Yo' know who I mean. It's him as wears no hat a lot!" I mean, some people shy away from it but I think it's a lovely part of the community, part of the culture. The industry's brought about a special breed of person who'll certainly tell you what they think, and the humour can be a way of coping with unpleasant conditions, with persecution and danger in some cases

Swad's always been about the people. I mean, if you like, the camaraderie between miners and I presume, it would be the same camaraderie with people who worked in the pipe works. Times were hard, you banded together. You sort of worked like that. It was a depressive place, I suppose. The work was hard. People started work at some God forsaken hour in a morning, which I've forgotten about for years now.

You could tell a lad that had been raised in a mining village as soon as he went down the pit. It was something in him, something inherent. He *knew* without being told. He would have a good idea of how things should be done. It was remarkable. If you got someone from outside a mining area, they were as different as chalk and cheese. They could be trained, they could learn how to work underground but there wasn't that automatic knowledge that were bred in the local lads. It's an indefinable thing, part of the makeup and the whole area is steeped in it and you feel comfortable being here.

They used to fire these kilns, and salt 'em, what we call salt 'em, they put a glaze on 'em like. All the smoke used come in Swad. It were terrible. White smoke it choked ya. It got down your eyes and everywhere, but they finished with that you see. Some of 'em used to do it in a daytime, but when I worked at John Knowles's, they always salted a kiln at night, to save the smoke, so people wouldna get it so much.

If you look at it, the chapels, the churches, the choirs - all of them from mining communities. You got that togetherness there. In this area, it was Non-conformism more than the Anglican tradition. The chapels ran football teams, billiards and other activities. Each Sunday, week nights just the same, they'd be packed to the doors. They were places of worship, but places where you got all your social life too. One of the things that came out of it was, in its nicest sense, a form of socialism. A lot of the Trades Union movement came out of Non-conformism, as did some of the most eloquent politicians and speakers. Some had trained as preachers and they could talk. They knew what they were talking about and they had the backing of the community.

There are plenty of more salubrious places, not too far away but they don't have the atmosphere. Whether it's to do with the comradeship that you gained in the pits or being part of a pit community, I don't know. Other industries don't have it. They would like to think they do, but they don't. It's because you've gone down that pit and it sounds a bit melodramatic but you've faced dangers together. That's what it is. You've been born into it, brought up in it, bred in it. You don't acquire it, like a new jacket, it's just there. A feeling of oneness.

The mining attitude's still here. I feel more at home in Swad than I do anywhere. Even now, though it's pedestrianised, all the area outside the old town hall and even though the Delph has changed - no market now - the people haven't changed. They're still on the seats, forming little enclaves and discussion groups. Many of them are ex-miners and as time passes, it's bound to change but that togetherness still remains. Now there are no pits to talk about, they've got different subjects - football being one of the most passionate! I walked into a newsagents in Swad last week, and there stuck in front of me were a Leicester City Sports paper and I smiled and said to the wife, "Now, there's some arguments for the Delph!"

When I come into Swad on a Saturday morning and someone shouts at me - and it's not many minutes before that happens, they'll shout, "Ay up! 'Ow are ye doin'?" and I turn to my wife and say, "I'm at 'ome" and that's true.

A terrible road to get your bread

 For men, facing danger was every day,
And the waiting women had a price to pay.

One of my memories of Castle Gresley was of the steam winding engine at Cadley Hill Colliery. This piece of machinery wound the cage with the men in up and down the shaft, from the pit bottom to the surface. Supplies also went down this way and coal was brought to the surface using this method. We could hear the sound of the winding gear from our bedroom windows half a mile away on Burton Road. The noise became part of our lives, we could set our clocks by the sound of the whistle blowing for the men's knocking off time and also the start of a new shift.

As a lad in the mid-fifties I liked to walk through the pit yard and gaze into the different workshops at the pit head. There was the fitting as well as the electrical shop but what charmed me the most and drew me like a magnet was the blacksmith's shop. To watch the red hot metal being moulded into different shapes and made into equipment for use down the mine absolutely fascinated me.

Another exciting thing was to go into the field and feed the pit ponies when they were brought up to the surface at holiday times. The ponies seemed to enjoy this break from the pit bottom, jumping and skipping and eating the carrots which we brought along to feed them. The pit became part of our lives. We used to watch for the night shift men coming off and walking home on a Friday, they would buy chocolates and sweets to take home for a treat.

It was a happy time but also there were sad times, particularly when one morning we heard the sound of knocking at the front door. My gran with whom I lived as a lad, went to the door and opened it. Outside stood some National Coal Board officials, I could see that they were all dressed in suits. It appeared that the husband of a friend of my gran had been killed during the night shift and they wanted her to go with them to break the awful news. This scarring memory remained deep-seated and in some way helped to shape the course of my life. Little did I know that morning that within a few years I would start my working life at Cadley Hill Colliery, later transferring to Donisthorpe. Eventually I became NUM lay official and was active in the difficult traumatic times which the coal industry went through.

To be honest, it was very hard work, when you worked your way through haulage work and got onto the coal face. You had a pick, a shovel and a hammer and you had to fill seven yards of Woodfield coal as they called it which could have been five foot high, four feet depth of cut and seven yards long. You used have to get the fireman to fire shots in it and you had to fill it out on the conveyor belt which took it to the pit bottom and then up the shaft in boxes. We never carried a lot of fat on us then. We were all lean. I were talking to Eric Langley the other week and I said, "We had some work then, Eric, didn't we?" and he said, "Arr, we looked like bloomin' whippets."

We worked a stocking seam which was a bit higher than the Kilburn seam and of course I had to go down there with cutters, the conveyors and haulages and keep them going. Some men never saw daylight in the winter months. We went on in the dark and came off in the dark. There could be thirty men on a coal face, all working with pick, shovel and hammers. If one man was on a rough patch, say a faulty area, the others would help him out if he was behind, so everybody had more or less finished at the same time.

The first bloke'd get in the pub. Let's imagine that he'd been on the day shift on a particular face and before baths came into being. He'd say, "I'll see you in the pub then youth, tonight!" and he'd come in and say, "How did they go on, so and so?" "Oh, didny'a hear? B.... chain broke!" "It didner!" "It did - afternoon shift's mekkin up for it, they're stoppin', workin' through snap." This is how it used to go. There'd be dominoes and it'd be like, "Right, deal him in", the pints'd be coming around and it's no exaggeration to say that the performance on that particular face, at that particular pit, would be of more importance than the game of dominoes or indeed how the beer tasted that night. There were some plans made in pubs and some problems overcome because suggestions used to be flung out. One colliery manager told me, "I had this problem. I thought it were insurmountable." I got my pipe on and before I'd got it going, the lads had sorted it, the problem had solved itself. A wise man once said to me, "Don't say, 'We're gonna do this...' Say to your men, 'I got a problem and I dunna know how to solve it,' and within five minutes they'll tell you how, and not only that. Because they've told you how, they'll go and do it too." True words.

It's pee dee terdee me butty,
Thony dee a miner smiles
Counting the notes in 'is packet
As 'e's standin' in ragged files,
Checkin' 'is slip ter say if 'e's short.
New tally system's nowt but a racket
Bin devised to get us all caught.

Workin' all wik till Satdee nate
thony bit o' pleasure a workin' mon 'as
When 'e gus ter the pub fer 'is pint,
Ter talk to 'is mates 'bout 'orses,
'Ar it wer only jus' beat by a neck
I'd er 'ad ten quid in me pocket
The lousy jockey! 'e 'elt it in check.'

An' young Jimmy's 'opeless, did yer say that goal,
Yis, are see it niver ought ter bin gen
'Cos when arn 'ad me 'ole Satdee dinner
Ar could plee miles better mesen.
Thole bloomin' team they want scrappin'
New blood's what thay want me lads
but it dunner matter 'ow the younguns plee
They'll niver bay as good as their Dads.

George was a tall good looking man with a mop of blond wavy hair, and eyes of blue which were enough to fetch the ducks off the water. He was a miner by trade, as had been generations before him. When working down the coal mine, he was a high spirited man, who could turn out "pit talk" as good as the rest. I think he would definitely have been seen "as one of the boys."

Friday, like with most of the miners was George's favourite day, and in his eyes it was the only day he felt he got paid for. On this special day he would hang up his talley before leaving the pit and pick up his wages along with his work mates. Then follow custom of counting and recounting his money to make sure he had not been short changed. When the miners had all checked their money and goodbye's had been exchanged, George would make his way to the local shops.

It was getting quite a ritual for George to go shopping on a Friday, and his sole aim was to buy something really special for his wife to wear. What would it be today? Last week it was a very lacy pair of knickers but this week he had his eye on a very beautiful underskirt. This garment had been the feature in the shop window for the best part of the week. In his mind he could already see the picture of sheer delight on his wife's face should he be lucky enough to buy it. She loved and adored new clothes and he felt this article was a "real cracker."

Soon he was approaching the ladies' outfitters shop. The proprietor, as usual, was almost at the door to greet him. Exchanging pleasantries and asking of her good health, not a trace of "pit talk" to be heard. In the company of women, he did not lack charm as he spoke and made gestures of politeness that would convince any woman that she was the "Bee's Knee's." Within moments the undergarment would be whisked away from the window display. He never touched the garment, only admired it from afar. This was due to the fact that he feared getting coal dust all over it, as bath time after working down the pit did not take place until he got home. Once he reached home his wife would be waiting with lashings of hot water and the old tin bath placed as near to the roaring coal fire as it would go. Due to the fact that his shopping visits were so often the proprietor was fully acquainted with the size fitting required. More often than not he would purchase the garment and with brown parcel tucked proudly under his arm he would make his way down the bank in eagerness to get home. However, if he was not successful in making a purchase, all was not lost, as his wife also liked perfume. Therefore, his next port of call would be the chemist to smell the delights they had on offer.

On his return home everywhere in the house would look spotlessly clean and the aroma of lavender polish would penetrate the air. Friday was always the day when the house was turned out from top to bottom in readiness for any relatives or visitors that may be passing by. His wife was always highly delighted by her fortune, but in which way she thanked him... well, I have no idea! All I know is that she could often be seen whispering quietly to her very close friends telling them of her gifts, but never as far as I know did any of George's friends know of his Friday afternoon expeditions.

I didna mind nights 'cos for the wife like, I could come home in a mornin', and I could see me children. Well, I used just have a bit of breakfast, and then go to bed. The

I remember when we had visitors up from St Ives. We'd met them on holiday actually, and we got quite friendly with them, and they came up. I said, "Did you find your way alright?" and they said, "Well eventually, but My God!", he said, "I'd no idea such places existed." I said, "What do you mean?" He said, "It's such a filthy area, if you don't mind me saying so. The streets were sludged up with clay when we came through. Cottages splashed up with clay, and black with smoke. I can't believe it that you live in these conditions up here." I said "I know, we live in 'em and work in 'em as well. The conditions are terrible in these pipe yards and brick yards. It's very hard dirty work, and the collieries as well, they have terrible conditions to work under." He was really surprised.

children used come home about what, 4 o'clock, half past four. I could get up then, and we used all have us dinner together then, have a bit of a chat and then I were more or less ready for work.

I never used to see me children on afternoon shift. You never seen hardly anyone. Sometimes if I were stoppin' overtime and different things, I mean, it used be one and two o'clock in a mornin' I'd land 'ome and then the children naturally were in bed and the wife and I used go to bed. When they got up in the mornin' for school, I never used see 'em. They'd just come and kiss me in bed and say "We're going school, Dad" and then when I went out, I used go out of the house about one o'clock, on afternoon shift.

A Bevin boy was someone who'd been called up initially, to serve in the forces. We were all given a number, and depending on what that number ended in, you were chosen to go down the pit instead. Lots of the lads protested, as I did, because I wanted to be in the territorials like me dad, but they wouldn't let me in.

I had to go to a place just outside Sheffield, Little Woodhouse Colliery. It was for a medical, and after that, the first thing they did was issue us with a pair of hob nailed, steel capped pit boots, a helmet and moleskin trousers. Then they took us on a fifteen mile hike to get us used to the boots, but when we got to the nearest pub, they couldn't move us any further.

I was assigned to Boardman's Pit, Swadlincote, and they had their own way of initiating us to the cage. We used to flash our helmet lamps to the engine winding man, and he knew then that there was a new comer on the cage. He lifted it up off the stocks about eight feet and just dropped it! It was quite an experience with the wind whistling by your ears and all the coal dust flying. You had to close your eyes and put fingers in your ears. One poor soul in particular fainted when he got to the bottom, and he wouldn't go down again. They had to employ him on the top, but I must admit I quite enjoyed it.

We had a tin to put our sandwiches in. It was shaped like a round topped door, with a handle, and it split in two. It was called a snap tin. We also had an enamelled water bottle, and both could be fastened on the belt with a hook.

I did my time at the pit - three years, two of which I spent driving the main haulage motor at the Kilburn seam without any accidents - and that wasn't easy. All your weight was balanced on two brakes. You were standing on two foot brakes, and you had to hold onto the emergency brakes with each hand. There were two drums, and you were operating both at the same time, lowering one a time under the coal loader, which was a belt loading the tubs. You had to lower the full train of twenty-five tubs, each containing a ton. You were lowered down into the pit bottom with your left leg on one brake drum, and lowering one at a time on the other leg.

You had two separate bells with different tones each side of your ear, and you had to listen intently sometimes, because the noise of the trucks going by the motor house was deafening at times. I used to come home many a day with my ears ringing.

One day we had a bit of trouble. They were carrying a bore hole in the coal, about fifteen feet, because they were hoping to miss Nadin's Pit Shaft. But unfortunately they miscalculated the direction, and the water broke in, and everyone had to literally run for their lives. We were up on top for three weeks, digging a trench two feet deep, right up to Nadin's Colliery. An armoured cable had to be put in to take more electricity to Nadin's old pit shaft, to put more pumps into the shaft to clear the water. It took us three weeks to do it, and it was quite a while before there was any effect felt, and the pump started to gain ground. Anyway, I enjoyed being on top for a while. We had the best of the summer weather, and I even got a suntan in the bargain.

Nobody would believe we were miners, because we didn't go home black at the end of the day. Well, you can't blame 'em - whoever heard of a miner with a suntan?

Let me tell you about my Grandad. He was a Newhall lad, who at the age of eleven, went to work with his father and Grandfather, in a pit that went under Swad Recreation Ground. I think it was Oldfield's Colliery, called 'The Old Shoddy' by local people.

Young lads started work doing jobs like - opening ventilation doors, and brattis sheets, to let the pony trains through - working by candlelight. The sheets would be replaced afterwards. Pony driving was the next step up the ladder.

This particular day, Tom was doing his job when water started to pour along the floor. He found a ledge to stand on, but the water was soon rising past his waist. To make things worse, the candle went out, leaving him in pitch black darkness. At a loss what to do, he just stood there. He heard the voices of men making their way out of the pit, and called out to them but nobody replied; it was every man for himself. Then he heard voices that he recognised. "Take me with you, Grandad!" he shouted, and he came out of the pit in total darkness, riding on his Grandad's back (the old men could get about in darkness, by sliding one foot along the tram rails). In his adult years, he worked at Nadin's Colliery, down the Oversetts, and progressed to the position of Stallman. This put him in charge of employing and paying his team of workers.

He set a filler on, one particular week and being in the dark days of winter, when they only saw daylight at weekends, it was not until paying out time that he saw his new worker in the light of day, and it was then that he realised it was a woman. The law at that time forbad the employment of women in mines, and I guess it must have been with mixed feelings that she had to finish.

In his early days of mining the electric cap lamps had not been invented so miners like my mate Jim relied on the locked flame safety lamp, giving no more light than a candle. When the flame was accidentally knocked out, finding his way to the re-lighter station in complete darkness was hazardous, but it was a great help to have his pony that could guide him about in the pitch black darkness. Not only did the pony save him time, but if he could keep his head below the height of the pony, it would save him from hitting his head on the low roof supports. In Jim's own words it was very painful to keep running your head into the low roof supports with only a soft cloth cap for protection.

I asked Jim if he had ever been scared while working in the pits. "O yes, several times," he replied. Some of it happened at a pit that was nicknamed the suicide pit. Tragic events varied from men getting crushed with runaway wagons to oxyacetylene cutters used in the pit to separate wagons after major accidents that frequently occurred on the very steep inclines.

He was always scared when he witnessed the coal cutter machine cable being used to set off explosive shot firing charges. The ultimate for Jim was when he was leaving a two feet high coal face; after completing his stint he started to crawl on his hands and knees to get to the main roadway. As he crawled forward he could see the roof support sinking in the floor, letting the roof drop down at an alarming rate leaving very little room for him to crawl under. As he went forward, he could see the roof dropping down but carried on in a desperate attempt to get from under the crushing roof. By this time he could feel the roof pressing on his back then sheer panic took over. He admits that he thought he was going to die under the crushing roof and it was only a last desperate attempt to squeeze his body from under the falling rock that saved his life. To this day he hates to think about it but he is not ashamed to tell you that at the time he screamed in fear of losing his life.

One's first experience of an underground emergency can be put on the same level as a parachute jump. All the training you do is very hard but the final crunch is the moment

My dad worked at Stanton Pit. On Friday the pitmen got paid, and the wives used to wait at home with their clean pinnies on, for the money. It wasn't much in them days. Dad only earned £3 something, and he was a deputy. There was always someone else who waited for the pitmen to be paid, and that was the man who sold pitboots, and ordinary shoes. The wives used to give him 6d a week (2½p).

when you have to do it for real. All the old miners I knew supported their fellow workmen in a number of ways. Charlie Waterfield comes to mind as a leader of men. Not only was he known as a comic character in a desperate situation, but he would carry out work in the most dangerous roof conditions to make it safe for his men to work under, he would take risks without any regard for his own safety.

I was with Charlie on one occasion where a miner injured his leg and as always with a suspected bone fracture the patient was never allowed to walk on it. This brought the best in Charlie as he was a keen Saint John's Ambulance Officer so this task to him was no problem. After treating the patient, Keg, and making him comfortable, a gang of six stretcher bearers set out on their long trek to the pit bottom.

They set off full of enthusiasms on their walk with Charlie in charge; at the start it seemed easy but with Keg being overweight and walking up a long incline it soon took its toll on all the stretcher bearers, stopping more frequently to get their breath back. As always Charlie took more than his fair share of the work and started to wilter fast to the extent that he stopped the men even more frequently for a well earned rest.

It was at one of the rest periods that Charlie's character showed up the best. When he had regained his breath he found a small clear space on the floor, dropped on his knees, put his hands together and out loud said a little prayer. "Lord, if you ever make another one like Keg, please put wheels on him." It was an act that lifted everyone's morale, something that only Charlie could do on the spur of the moment, while in a difficult situation. I found him a genuine man and easy to work with - if he could not remember your name, he would call you brother, in fact everyone was brother to Charlie.

On another occasion when I came into contact with him there was a serious accident where a large roof fall had buried two men. One of them was trapped underneath a rock pile with only his head not covered but the weight on his body made it difficult for him to breath. It was his mate's immediate action to stop the dribbling rock covering his head that saved him from suffocation. The other victim could not be seen at all but help to try and find him was soon available. Charlie was told about the accident in another part of the mine and soon made his way to us, and with sleeves rolled up dived into action clearing the rock fall, working under what was the most dangerous roof conditions. When it was brought to Charlie's attention that he was under loose rock which could fall on him at any moment, he replied, "It'll be alright, let's get him out."

It was a slow operation to move the fallen rock: to use a pick or a shovel could cause further injury so all the digging was done with our bare hands. While the first man was now being stretchered to the surface the other one had not been found, creating anxiety as to what sort of condition we were going to find him in. An oxygen reviver unit had been sent for from the surface so that we could administer oxygen as soon as he was uncovered. Concern for this man's safety was illustrated by the arrival of the colliery manager Mr Reid, followed closely by Dennis Crane and Bill Dennis with a reviver unit.

Their efforts were nulled by the fact that the buried man had not been located. It was fast approaching half an hour's constant digging when some one yelled out, he is here. At this moment it was Charlie that took over clearing the patient's face and prepared him for artificial respiration. I was the only one amongst us trained to administer oxygen with the reviver unit so it was no trouble to get the patient coupled up straight away. Charlie started the Holger Nielson method of artificial respiration, after a while it became clear by the fluctuation of the breathing bladder he was making our patient take in oxygen. By this time the Overseal Doctor Erwin arrived on the scene; all activity stopped while he examined our patient. His words were, "You can do no more, lads," and pronounced life extinct. Charlie gave me the opinion that he had been through all this before but the doctor's words shattered me both mentally and physically and the silence that followed said it all for the others.

The devotion shown to the dead man in the hour long struggle to save him carried on in earnest. A team of men collected together to form another stretcher party with Charlie at the helm they set off on a long walk to the pit bottom. On the surface arrangements had been made by Joe Redfern, the afternoon SRN to receive the body at the mortuary, a small gothic style looking church sited next to the Rawdon winder house. Joe was another devoted man that cared for the welfare of others dealing with accident victims of all descriptions and this incident was nothing new to Joe.

On several occasions he called upon myself to assist him in the mortuary to wash and manoeuvre bodies on the narrow slab. What struck me about Joe was the pride and the sincerity on him to maintain their dignity. Joe always appeared to be a rough and ready type of fellow but it was at times like this that I found Joe to be a caring person to do his best to ease the pain of the grieving families. In the coal fields, there were lots of men like Charlie and Joe, too many to mention, with one aim in life, which was to help their fellow men.

Well anyroad
Oh me mam lay on the sofa and went to sleep
and all at once she jumped up
and asked, "Where's your Dad?"

I says: "He's been shouting good night kid to you,"
and I says, "He's gone."

So, anyroad,
she didner tell us.
We all went to bed.

And she heard –
this is the night
he gets killed.

Well, she was praying
all night.
She got to bed but she didn't sleep.
She was up next morning.
She got the fire going and the lights on
and they brought me dad home
by ambulance.

He had his foot trapped
but some of them who were with him
said it was the biggest wonder out
as Mr Harrison wonna killed
with the stone that had come down.
And it's terrible road to get your bread.

It was 2 - 3 o'clock in the morning before I ever went to sleep. It was always a worry that he was there. I was waiting for him to come home, when I'd finally dropped to sleep. I'd never been in a mining town before and to marry a miner it was a big thing -

to know what they went through down the pit, 'cos I know other times there've been tragedies down there. One of his mates died down the pit, and Reg had only just started back after having a heart attack himself, and he came home. Let him tell you the story...

'**I** were on afternoon shift then. We'd just landed there, I were working down in the stone heads. There were no deputy there, nor nothing, 'cos when you were contracting, you used mek haste and get to your job, so's you could start and earn your money, and they'd left the Panzer chain fast. There were three of us in the heads.

Jim sat down and had orange and he says, "Aren't you having anything, Reg?" and I says "No, I had a big dinner." But most of the miners when they land there, they usually have their snap, and then they work through all the shift. They dunna bother about food agen.

So anyroad, I went and checked this Panzer chain, and I found it were slack. There's what you call the links on a chain, and the flights, and I could find out if the chain were slack, so I said, "It wants three's in and tek five's out links, and put three's in." So anyroad, he jumped up on this Panzer chain, and I got me spanner and was undoing one side, and Jim, me mate, he jumped up. He says, "You find your three thread," he says, 'cos we used hide 'em down the Pit, and anyroad, I says, "Leave that pin in there," I says, "and it'll help you tek your t'other one out."

Well, he'd just got the spanners and pulled 'em. He goes, "Oh!" And that were it, he'd gone! There were no deputy nor nothing there, and I 'adna got much knowledge of first aid, but I knowed a bit, I mean, one of me daughters she's a midwife. She's been a Sister at Burton Infirmary, so I mean, you talk about it in the family, so I started mouth to mouth on him, I just said to my other mate, "undo his belt." Well you could tell he'd gone. Anyroad, he says, "I can't get his belt off, Reg," so I said, "Get my Stanley knife out me bag, and cut if off." So he cut his belt off, 'cause when you're on a Panzer chain, it's bloomin hard on there. He took his belt and his self rescuer and his battery, and pulled that from underneath him, but I'd already started mouth to mouth on him. But it were no good.

We'd got what they called the Beethoven battery. That's what blowed the heads down, so I couldn't do anything with trying to bring him round. I'd heard about these 'lectric shocks, so I put some wires round his wrists and on to the battery, and you used have to wind the battery up, and I were just about ready for pressing the button. It would have burnt his bloomin' arms, but I didna know any different and I wanted bring him round, but then the ambulance man came saying, "What you doin', Reg?" "I'm trying get him bloomin round." He came and checked him and said, "There's nothing you can do."

The Sister come down then, 'cos it'd tek about three quarters of an hour for get down the Pit on the paddies and different things. "There's nothing we can do, Reg," her says. "He's gone." So we brought him out, and I come out with him, and me mates. Anyroad, he'd gone, so the Sergeant come to me, and we went and had a cup of tea in the canteen. The Sergeant says, "Please would you identify him if his wife don't want to." I said. "Ooh arr." Anyroad, poor Jim. I mean, we had us happy times.

A decree came out from, not Caesarea but Hobart House to put on what came to be known as safety sketches. Safety was always top of the list of the Board's priorities. My manager gave me this task, to organise and so I started pulling people in, to get a team together. The objective was you wrote, produced and acted everything. The rules were that you had to have all the people involved, from the pit. They could be an engineer or telephonist but they had to be working at the pit. Actually, you were allowed one other person that had to be married or a relative of someone at the pit. We had Molly and she was a semi-professional singer. The theme had to be safety in the mine but you could do anything you liked so long as you got your message through in an entertaining way. Bits of paper would be floating about and verses would be coming from here, there and everywhere. We used to meet in our local chapel halls and village halls and we'd finish up at the pub. When the colliery club got off the ground, we met there. It was a national initiative and there was a national competition with each pit able to submit a team that could enter. Our team got through to the national finals at the New London Theatre, Drury Lane in London. You'd be judged by how many safety points you was making, along with acting ability and audience reaction. Even though a lot of the dialogue had technical pit terms, the audience were all miners and their families so the reaction was always wonderful.

A lot of thought and energy went into the sketches. We all dressed up. One of the funniest sights was Albert as a fairy. We made him this wand from a hollow piece of plastic and we got the blacksmith to make us a metal pan and we got charge on this pan and of course it went off wi' a flash and a cloud of smoke. It'd leave Albert peering out of this cloud with him in all his fairy gear. I once stood too near and when the explosive charge went off, it nearly blew me through t'other side of the stage. I'd run a piece of elastic through the rod so while he got the elastic taut, the rod was taut and the star'd stay

You could post notices up in the covered accomodation at the pit until you were blue in the face but nobody would bother with them. They'd pass them by. So these little sketches were a light hearted way to get home a very serious message - the need to be safety conscious in every part of the working day. They were clever, you weren't being preached at but you were being entertained.

up. 'I am the Queen of Fairyland N.C.B division!' and the rod'd bend. Used to have everyone in stitches. I remember spraying his pit boots with silver lacquer and this tinsel stuff and that women'd put in their hair. Do you remember Alastair Yates from Radio Derby? He'd come to interview us in the conference room at Donisthorpe Pit. Albert was unusually quiet, hardly saying anything and in the end he goes, "It's no good, I just can't do it without the wand."

One of our best sketches involved Baron Frankenstein and we got Frankenstein to hunt for pieces of bodies to complete his monster. The accidents that we went through enabled him to get various pieces of body parts. We got the monster behind a semi-circular cage affair, curtain round it and electric light bulbs all around. The audience couldn't see what was in it until the monster came out. Harry McPherson, deputy manager, was volunteered to act as the monster. We bought this mask from some theatrical people in Leicester. It'd even got the bolt through it and it was most horrific. The rest of him was covered in an old sheet that had been torn and we made his body up to look like it had been badly burned. Ivan recorded a special tune for the monster and by some strange coincidence only the bass came out and it sounded smashing – ever so spooky. To this day, he doesn't know how he did it. Anyway, it's still crystal clear in my mind and I'll do you a bit….

Imagine the scene. Empty stage. Telephone ringing. Des Jackson rushes in to pick up phone.

Des: Alright, alright, I can hear ye. What? Oh, Coroners Office, oh, hello Sergeant Smith. Yep. Yep. Got that. Inquest been fixed for when? Next Wednesday? Yep, you're right, it is tragic. Weight of the fall? Forty tons, I reckon. Yep. OK. I'll see you. Cheers.

Puts phone down.

(Thinks aloud) Fourteen fatalities from falls a'ground and now this. We've had more falls than the bank rate. Let's see what 'is mate 'ad to say. (Looks through accident statement) Thought so. Looked as sound as a bell, was it 'ell! If there'd been a damn great crack, he'd have protected his back. Temporary support? Hah! Another last thought! I'd sell my soul if I thought they'd reduce blasted figures.

Gets down statistics chart off the wall. Knock on the door.

Des: Come in!

Arnold Webster and Bill Kirby enter the room.

Arnold: Morning! You sent for us, I think?

Des: Yep. I want to go over those statements on that fatality – the one that happened to that electrician, Willie Battersby. It's said he worked without due care.

Bill: Ay. He looks like Jimmy Cagney and sings like t'electric chair.

That's the one. If only he'd carried his permit to work and his isolate and check, he'd be now alive and well y'see. What the hell's that?

Lorry goes past window. (We got this rigged up backstage with a model of a top cab of a lorry). Screech of brakes as Des goes out of the room.

Arnold: What a job! I'd rather be on t'dole. No wonder he said he could sometimes sell his soul.

There's a bang and a green flash on stage. Ivan stands there, deathly white in a frock tail coat.

Ivan: Souls for sale, I hear you say?

I'll make sure this one doesn't get away.

Just lend me your willing ears,

I'll soon remove your doubts and fears.

Just let things slide, don't wear a frown

I'll tip your statistics upside down.

Off-Stage the statistics chart tips up so it looks as if the accident rate is coming down.

Arnold: Who the bloomin' 'ell's this? 'ee looks rate rough.

Don't look at me. He's no friend of mine!

Ivan: At your service, gentlemen. Baron Frankenstein!

We'd got overtime ban at the time, and I'd gone out on afternoon shift and we'd heard as there was a fire there. When I got there they sent all the contractors to this fire. We were putting a stoppin' on. The day shift had started it, so we had to continue; we was teking one another off, and then, the rescue team wasn't there at the time, we're putting this stoppin on and some of them, I don't know who it was now, opened the top where the laggin' is and it was really blazing up there.

The manager were there and we were on this stoppin' and then smoke comes out behind us, about thirty yards and we all rushed back into the fresh air again. We'd got our hoses going. We could have got out with us self rescuers, we could 'ave put them on, but that's what they say. Self rescue, it's for nothing else. It's for yourself. Then the rescue team came, and we were doing what we could, as managers instructed us what to do with the hoses and different things. Then one of the managers said to come to one of the rescue team. "Get all your tackle on and go into the fire, into the smoke, and

find out where the heart of the fire is." So they go, with all the tackle on, whilst one of them rigged a piece of rope tied to him, and he went out into the fire. You couldn't see him, but you'd got your hoses working that road, and you could hear this squarker going...Quark..quark..quark..quark..quark. But all at once, I reckon he'd only gone about twenty yards: Quark, Quark, Quark, Quark. He come back again. He couldna get to the heart of the fire. So they had to go in the return and fetch all the face men off, and that was a brand new face an' all, as it had just kicked up. They lost no end of tackle at Cadley Hill, through the fire.

What they did, you see, they blocked it all off. They put the stoppin' on in the main airway, and in the return as goes round, they just blocked it all off. That were all completely finished with then. There were thousands of pounds lost there.

I think there were a lean horse machine down there as well, as I used to drive. All this was lost. All this tackle, the whole lot.

It'd go out, they said. In time it'd go out on itself, then they'd tek samples. They'd then got pipes through were you put this stoppin' on, and they tek samples see if fire's still burning or what, you see. But mostly the deputies they go and check regular down there. There was a lot of money lost, helluva lot of money.

Well, there were no people. They all got out and they'd got other faces for to send the men on. The following day that were absolutely blocked off, and nothing could be fetched out the Pit on that side. It's still there now.

W‌hen I were on night shift, on a coal face, I were cutting, and I were with a bloke named Sid Tidsley. There were two of you to a machine, and we'd got two hundred and forty yard to cut, and you adna got much time for a comin' off, and 'avin' your snap and everything, so what you used do, you used 'ave a couple of rounds before you went on the face; start the machine and get the face cut before the men come on the day shift if possible.

Mostly, you could get it done but you were working all the time. I can remember one of my mates were just running the machine round. When you turn the machine round, there were a big piece of coal come off and it caught his leg. Well, there were only me and him there. Black as it was, I took his breeches down, and all his thigh was black, it was absolutely black where the coal had caught him, and I got on the tannoy to the deputy.

Coming up into the coal face, you'd got to walk up. It were one in four, as you'd got

My little daughter Tina used like have a joke with me. Once, when I was stone heading I opened me snap tin down the Pit and one of my mates said, "What you got in your snap tin, Reg?" Well there were a little letter and it had got, 'My darling, I love you and I miss you more than anything.' I know'd who'd done that. It were Tina, meant as her mum and she used put one or two little letters in but it used mek me a bit embarrassed when some of the men were all sitting down. "Ooh, look at Reg again with his letters! Arr!" and they'd all laugh.

to go in, so Sid Tidsley, him as 'ad got hurt, I just pulled him off. Got him out from under the coal and he says, "Give me a drink of water," so I said, "No, you're not supposed have water when you're hurt." He says, "Look, they've changed the law now. Give me my bottle. Let me have a drink of water." But I told 'em bring the stretcher.

Well, he wudna get on this stretcher, Sid wudna. They got him down to the belt, and they rode him out on the belt, and when they got him at the other end, they got a trolley there as they used to tek you the pit bottom, but I think as they were teking him off the belt, they caught hold of his wrong leg. They caught hold of his bad leg, and he bloomin' screamed, old Sid did, but I wanna there, I were only going on what these other men had told me. I stopped on the coal face.

I started work at fourteen in the blacksmith's shop in Cadley Hill Colliery in November, 1941. The shop had no natural light, the windows had been painted out for the blackout; this was the third winter of the war. Still, we were as well off for light as many of the shops in High Street, Swadlincote, which had corrugated iron windows with the words - business as usual painted on them. Davenport's wine shop will be remembered by many, having the words - our windows did not stand the test, but you'll find our spirits still the best - painted on the zinc.

Anyway, back at the blacksmiths, I asked if I could use the 14lb sledge hammer instead of the 7lb backing hammer. The reply was: "There is never a horse born, but what there is a collar to fit." Nothing to do with me or the hammer, but I got the message.

There were four blacksmiths, each with a teenage youth as a striker, and at snap time it was usual to sit in a group, not only to eat but to discuss everything. One thing I learned, was that Cadley had thirty ponies and during the period between wars, the number had been as many as ninety, "What happens to the old ponies?" I asked. "Are they sold?" "No they're put down before they are taken away," was the reply and then I was given a reason as to why this was done.

One day, on reaching retirement age, one of the ponies was taken home by one of the pit owners, for the use of his children. All went well, until the day when the pony and trap, with the kids in it, were on the Trent Bridge at Willington. The pony became startled by the traffic and tried to get off the road and into the river. It was a frightening experience for the kids, and put an end to using pit ponies after they had retired.

Another pony story was about four deputies who were going to do some underground

In the very old days at the pits, they had a shop at the pit top and they didn't pay you in money, they paid you in tallies and them tallies were redeemable in that shop at their prices and that's where you got everything from. They called them Tommy Shops.

roadway repairs, on a day when the pit was not turning coal. They chose a quiet pony from the stables, one that would walk without being led. They tacked it up and dogged it on to a box or tram.

After putting their tools in the box, all four climbed in and set off towards the place where the work was to be done. They sat there, riding along, when the pony stopped. After several "go-ons", there was the sound of cracking timber and the roof ahead of the pony fell in, blocking the roadway. The cries of "go-on" changed to "back, back" and four men were very grateful for the thing called horse sense.

Sadly, a pony died on the night shift and was sent up the pit to the surface. The smith I was working with suggested that we take a look at it. There was little to be seen of any injuries and the shoes were removed for re-use and I think that was the sole purpose of our visit.

Many people have the opinion that horses have no sense, but anyone who has worked down a coal mine with ponies can dispel that idea all together. A pit pony would only work when it wanted to work.

They could be crafty by working much harder if you gave them a sweet; sometimes for a treat a pony would look forward to the crust off your sandwiches, but better than that, if you had an apple packed up for your lunch it would pester you until it had all been eaten.

A young teenage pony lad would not give the pony any of his lunch but the older men would share their food more liberally.

Each pony was an individual and like a dog would carry out a trick to gain a sweet. They would shake a paw- that's a hoof - when told to do so and roll back a top lip in preparation for a kiss. One pit pony I remember, called Snowy because of his pure white hair, had a particular novelty act. He would follow the driver by doing what he did on their return journey out of the district they worked in. On the way out the pony lad took the opportunity to ride on a low-lying man-rider belt. Not to be outdone, Snowy would follow suit by stepping up onto the belt and riding behind. It was a sight to see - Snowy standing on the conveyor, looking like the Trojan Horse.

Conditions changed dramatically after 1947 when the National Coal Board took over. All ponies had a log book to record the hours worked, to avoid a good pony doing more than an eight-hour shift without a long break in between. Their diet was also improved, with an abundant supply of fodder and water providing a good meal after every shift. Paintwork in the stables also changed. For many years the stable walls had been whitewashed with lime and water, but under new regulations introduced in 1947 all walls around the manger had to be changed to a pastel lime green. When the situation is given some thought you can understand the reasoning behind this. After spending an entire shift in complete darkness, to return to the reflection of electric lights on brilliant white walls would come as a great shock.

And ponies could, just like humans, bear grudges. If one was ill-treated it would not miss an opportunity to take revenge. It would wait for its assailant to walk on the narrow side of the tunnel then lean against him, pinning him to the side of the roadway. Then, for good measure, it would start to walk, rolling its victim round and round - it's a frightening experience to feel the weight of a pony's body crushing you into the roadway supports.

Welfare for the ponies eventually improved to the extent that when the miners had their two weeks' holiday, the ponies could come out of the pit for the same period. Getting them into the lift cage to enable this was often a hazardous experience. Several of them needed full eye covers whereas others would not require any special preparation at all. The latter gave you the impression they knew it was holiday time for them. Once in the lift cage they would start to whinny - something they rarely did - and when the cage left the pit bottom the tone would change to a higher pitch, as if to let the pony lads waiting for them at the top know they were on their way up.

The ponies from the nearby pits spent their two weeks' holiday in the Barratt Mill Fields set around the 20-acre stretch of water known as Barratt Mill Lake. Here they were under the watchful eye of Mr. John Jones, the head of the National Coal Board Forestry Department, having taken this job in 1911. On one occasion, when the ponies had been let loose, an individual galloped round the field so many times it dropped down from exhaustion and died.

In later years, as the pits started to use heavy machinery, it soon became obvious the loads were too much for the ponies to haul around and called instead for the use of rope-type haulages. It was in the 1961 to 1963 period that all ponies were withdrawn from the mines. They ended their lives in retirement, grazing in the fields they had roamed in during their two week holidays. The sight of the retired ponies grazing in the fields brought heart-felt sympathy from the public, many offering to take them into their own pastures for the rest of their days. No doubt it was a kind offer with good intent, but Mr. Morris Jones, the new forestry manager charged with the responsibility of caring for the ponies, would not let any one of them leave the Barratt Mills stables.

The proudest moment of my life was when I was told I had been picked to take my pony Dick to parade in front of His Majesty King George VI and Queen Elizabeth in the Windsor Great Park.

Two drivers from Granville and one from Netherseal pits were chosen out of a hundred or more drivers in the surrounding coal mines. The drivers George Atkins from Linton, Harry Redfern from Woodville and myself from Hartshorne were given the task of preparing our ponies a week before the parade.

To make the ponies more presentable the hoops had to be scrubbed many times, their coats and manes required constant grooming to get their coats to shine for the occasion. Not only was Dick given preferential treatment but all the other pony drivers were issued with grand new blue suits and a hard type safety helmet, a complete change from wearing an old cloth cap.

On the day of the journey to London, the train picked up a number of ponies at Ashby Railway Station and then carried on to stop at different stations going out as far as Durham.

We travelled in the same wagon with our ponies, three to a wagon feeding and watering them during the journey.

Arriving at London in the late afternoon we settled down to sandwiches and beer. Rows of wooden cabins had been put up for us to live in - little luxury!

The parade in front of His Majesty King George VI and Queen Elizabeth was enjoyed by everyone and to my surprise Queen Elizabeth showed a real interest in the pit ponies. Every day while the ponies stayed in London she made a point of visiting them as if they were something special to her. A small gesture that I'll never forget.

I used come home as black as the ace of spades, wi' shovelling coal and ashes and one mess and another. The only place they had a shower were on the yard.

From the ground to the table

When I left school, the Headmaster said to me, "Arr, young Sutton. Have you got a job?" And I said, "No, sir." "Well, before you leave school," he said, "Come and see me." So before I left, about a week to go, he came back and said, "They're wanting an apprentice at Farmers at Castle, and so," he said, "if you want the job, go down to Farmers, and tell 'em I've sent you. I've had a word with Mr Farmer." That was the old man who was one of the original founders of Farmer Brothers, and he lived at the corner of Swad Lane, Castle Gresley, and I said, "Thank you very much sir."

So, I went down to Farmer Brothers at Castle Gresley there in Station Street, and they said, "Oh yes, start to work on Monday." 'Course this was on the Friday after school I went down there. "Yes, start work on Monday. Be here at half past seven with a pair of overalls, and your pay will be ten shillings a week." Ten bob a week, in the old money, 50p today.

I started work as an apprentice, and my job first of all was mashing tea for all and sundry. Running jobs, doing little fiddly jobs for everybody who wanted a hand here and there and everywhere. That's where it all started.

From there I would learn turning using measuring instruments and going and helping the blacksmiths, going into the foundry and helping, all sorts of jobs, slowly building up engineering sort of interest, because Farmer's actually built brick and pipe machines and a lot of the firms round there had Farmers machinery, and so I stayed there about two years; but in that two years I'd done turning, blacksmith work, I'd helped in the foundry, done a bit of moulding, slowly building up what would be an engineering background. In fact, I've got the scars to prove it. I got fast in a machine lathe.

We had some good times. There were a lot of young apprentices during the beginning, the early part of the war and it was quite a lively place, as you can imagine, when they would lift somebody's car up and stick it between two double doors so the bloke couldn't get out with his car, and everybody else had scarpered off and disappeared, that sort of thing.

A lot of the stuff that they were on was war work, but they still had to do bits of machinery for their plant that they'd built - their pipe plants, and though I saw a certain amount of plant built, I never saw a complete Farmers' clay plant, which took in the raw clay, chopped it all about, did everything else and produced a pipe at the end of it.

We were a good team - the office staff at the Albion. We used enormous sized ledgers to write all the transactions in. I had a real job carrying them sometimes, but of course they were never as heavy as the pipes in the yard.

They were friendly times. The work was hard, it was dirty. It was hot, and looking back now, I'm often amazed that people did it, and they weren't paid a great deal. If you were pushing sixteen bob a week you were lucky, and you were probably working from six till five or six at night, and probably five and a half days a week.

I remember Swadlincote in the 1920's when the tram used to pass through the Main Street. There were few cars about, there were mostly lorries and carts pulling their loads. I have a vivid memory of the clay hole tucked the side of the road leading out of Swadlincote. No protection or anything, it was just a great big gaping hole where they'd been excavating the clay for the pipe yards.

I worked in one of the pipe yards when I left school at fourteen, and I went first of all into cleaning the hovels up with an old gentleman that worked there. Then I went on to the pipe machine, where I did what they call, the breaking out of the pipes, and also did the feeding job and the carrying off.

There were four main jobs on the pipe yard. The first stage was making pipes. This meant putting the clay into the machine, and keeping it stocked up with clay while the chappie down below was breaking the pipes out, and when he broke the pipes out he tipped it over to the fellow that was in charge of the gang, and he would fettle the pipe and then place it on to a tray to be carried away at the far end of the hovel to dry for several days. That was a really hard laborious job because we were on peace work. We had to do four or five hundred pipes a day to get anything like a reasonable wage.

From there I went into the brick hovels for a short while. That was worse than anything. The man was making the bricks by hand. He'd have a great pile of clay at the side of him, and on his table you would have a mould, and he'd scoop a great handful of clay and bang it on to the mould and level it off. I had to pick it up and run to the other end of the hovel and lay it down on the hot floor to dry, and get back again by the time he'd got another one ready.

It was a hard disagreeable job, and eventually, I left the pipe yard, and went to a shop called Hunters at Swadlincote and I was errand boy there.

It was uncomfortable especially in the brick works. The floor was so hot, and the drying space was quite a distance from where the bricks were made. We just dressed in shorts and a vest. Some of the lads didn't wear shoes, they'd run barefoot over the hovel's floor but I always wore a thin pair of shoes to protect me feet.

We'd got no facilities either. No men's room. In one corner there was an open urinal,

You had TG Green and Company. They produced whatsaname pots, drinking cups and all that. Then you'd got the sanitary ware. They produced toilets and urinals and them sort of things, different side of pottery.

and with the heat and that, it stunk terrible all over, you could smell it all over the area. Nowhere to sit apart from among the old rubbish to have your food at the break time. We used have about twenty minutes to eat our sandwiches, and have a drink of tea.

Conditions were dreadful on the Patent kiln. They used have to carry some of the chimney pots on to what we called the patent. They had it covered in, all over the top, and they used to use the top of the kiln for a drying room, and people had to carry six foot chimney pots on to this hot patent, and with being on top of kilns, the floor was so uneven and that, you had a job to walk properly carrying them chimney pots.

The kilns were fed from the top, they'd got little holes in the top and lids on and there was a chappie there with only one arm, the other arm was a metal one with a hook on the end. I believe he got it wounded in the first world war, and he had the job of hooking these lids off. The smoke and sulphur would come up from the kiln, and he'd hook two or three small shovels full of slack and stuff in to keep the fires going, and that all came puthering up into the area where you was, where you'd be carrying pipes and chimney pots to dry off.

One day there was an accident there. Not while I was there though, but years after, I heard about it: one of the kiln tops gave way, and this poor chap fell in. They tried to pull him out, but they could just get hold of his hand and arms and they were pulling flesh off his arms when they tried to pull him out, and of course it killed him but he was shouting a bit from the start. It was a terrible death that was.

I can remember going to the pipe works with me dad when I left school. Just before we got to the office, he met a fellow out of the clay hole that he knew, 'cos he lived in the same road as us, and he was having a chat with him, and I stood at the side waiting for him to have his chat with him, and I noticed the expression on the fellow's face, that me dad was talking to, when me dad was asking him questions - an expression of 'I wouldn't let him come here if I was you.' I could see he was frowning and shaking his head. "No," he says, "it's terrible here, I wouldn't like a lad of mine working here if I could help it." But we were so hard up you see, I had to tek the first job I could get hold of, and me dad took me to the office there and the yard manager had a look at me and asked me one or two questions, and could see that I was a big strong lad, and he says, "Yes, you can start on Monday."

It was a yard that they really were setting on and leaving 'em as fast as they set 'em on 'cos people couldn't stick it. It got a bad name. Albion pipe works were better. The one at Swadlincote, the Wraggs and Woodwards was a good firm to work for, but the conditions were about the same. But their standards were a little bit better than ours, the Ensors. It deteriorated there, really bad.

The first day I was there I went with the old man and I 'ad to go cleaning all the broken pipes up and that, and sweep the dust up and the clay and that, and put it in a scuttle there. He'd give me a lift up with it in a big scuttle, and he'd throw it on me shoulder, and I'd 'ave to trot off to the mill to have it ground up again, to be fed into the machine for making clay again, and at the end of the day, me shoulder was red raw, from this bloomin' old scuttle there and the weight of it and carrying it on me shoulder.

I was doing that for several days, and one day when the boss's son came looking round, I was sweeping the stairs down 'cos there was a double storey, and I had to sweep the clay and dust from one side so you could walk up, and I always remember - he smelt of perfume. He were a bit of a 'dandy' he was, and you could smell this perfume on him as he walked by. I mean, the actual smell there was terrible, but when he walked by, it was like a bit of fresh air coming by. I was on me hands and knees there, and I had to wipe this brushed bit on one side, so's he could walk up.

In the clay hole they had a man that were in charge of the gang that worked in the clay hole, and they'd got lines running down into the clay hole. It was so big, we had little ponies and trucks to go down into the clay hole, and as they were digging the clay out, they'd load it into these trucks and these ponies ad 'ave to pull it out.

I had about a week down there. I had to help to push the truck, because the little pony it was so old - it was so heavy, the load. A chap shouted to me and he says, "Eh, you!" he says. "You'll have that pony dropping. He's puffing too much. Have you oiled them wheels?", and I said "No. Nobody told me to oil them wheels, but they were greased, the wheels." They were fairly greased. "Grease them wheels a bit more," he said, "and you'll have to help him push." So I had to shout to the pony to pull and I used have to push the bloomin' wagon out of the clay hole.

I didn't stick that for long. I only had about a week of that, but it was terrible conditions down there. It was cold and wet. 'Course you had to work whether it was chucking it down or not, over the great clay hole there, and the others were digging the clay out. There was a chappie that was in charge of the gang, and he paid your wages out at the weekend.

I used to see the chappie that used to tram the clay that came up from the pug down below from the mill and it used to come up on this endless belt, and it used tip over at the top into a trolley, a truck for the chappie to tram it across to the different pipe machines and there was trucks all the way along, and all the way round. There was three pipe machines upstairs and two below on the ground floor.

He was right up above us. He used have to tram this clay from the mill, round to the machine and tip it up down a shute to where you was working to feed the machine. The machine had got a revolving paddle like a mincing machine and it squashed the clay down that you feed into this machine on this worm which pressed it down. But if the clay was a little too hard, it used churn up again, and you used have to keep pressing it down.

Well, the chappie in charge of this machine was down below me and he was the one that did the fettling when the pipes went through. I couldn't get the clay to go through, and they were coming down ever so slow, and they was on peace work, and he used keep shouting, "Fill the ****** up, and get cracking" and all that sort of thing. I got so aggravated with him one day, I'd got a little bucket at the side of me with water to splash the clay if it was too solid, to put into the machine and after all this shouting and swearing, I lost me temper, and I picked the bucket of water up and threw it all over him and he chased me all over the bloomin' yard.

Jobs that stuck in my memory was the kiln gang. Now the kiln gang was the chappies that used to collect the pipes out of the hovels. Carry 'em down the steps of the hovels across the yard into the kilns.

The chaps'd have p'r'aps five or six pipes, clay pipes piled on their shoulders up 'ere. No end of 'em had deformed shoulders with carrying their pipes, and they'd carry these pipes down through the hovels, down these steps across the yard out to the bloke inside the kiln, and it'd still be hot from the last lot of firing, and he'd be in there stacking them in the kiln, and they used to be going backwards and forwards like that all day. That was a really hard job.

I forget now how long they used to have to fire them for. I can well remember the chappie who used to fire round the kilns and he always looked as though he was singed up. He got no hairs on his arms and that, and he'd always got burns on him, because they had blow backs as well. They'd always got smoke coming out of 'em.

I used to come home from the pipe yards about 5 o'clock, and me mother'd have

We didn't have anything to help us from getting dirty. Protective clothing. Just an apron. It used to wrap over and tie. Salt's had always got plenty. You wore your ordinary clothes according to the weather.

me dinner ready for me, and then I'd curl up on the sofa and go to sleep, absolutely shattered. Then I'd wash and change and go out with the lads for a walk round, and laugh about anything. We did nothing out of the ordinary, we just coped by walking around and chatting with one another. We'd probably go to the pictures once a week and that was it. That was our lot in them days. We were satisfied with the smallest things in life. We used to try and make the best of it when we was away from work.

You wasn't classed as a pipe carrier until you had an egg on your shoulder. You see, a lump come up on your shoulder like an egg, and it stopped the pipes from slipping off. When I first started, and I used come home, my shirt used to be stuck to my shoulder with blood where it broke the skin, and once it healed and you said you had an egg - that was it - you were a pipe carrier.

I started to work at Wraggs and Woodwards in the early 1900s. At first I was in one of the machine gangs, feeding the machine, to make pipes. Then I went down below to carry them off and put them in the drying shed. It were really dusty, and there was a lot of noise. There were three pipe gangs, a big one, a middle one and a little one.

I was in the middle one, and it were really gruelling. I had to carry anything from two inch to twelve inch pipes on my shoulder, and I carried 'em from the hovels into the kilns, and I carried anything from eight, down to one, depending on size. I carried the 2 - 9 inch pipes on my shoulder, and one across the top of my head. I had a cap on.

When the pipes were fired and the kilns were finished, I had to draw them out again, and of course, they were hot, and the only thing I had were gloves, and I had to put them on my shoulder, bundles of them.

There was no canteen, nor nothing you see, but eventually they made a building into a canteen and a first-aid place. If you took any bacon or anything, you used to give it to the lady there, and she used to cook if for you. But my father was in the engine house. He looked after the engine, and of course he used to have a cooker there, and we'd cook ours in there.

We started at half past seven, and finished at five o'clock, then I had to go back home to Newhall on my bike, or walk it if I'd got a puncture.

The tubs used to come down from Granville on a steel rope, and there were four come altogether. They used to come rumbling down, and you had to watch yourself when they were emptying the kiln, because we had to cross the railway lines, and at the

'Over the years, some have met a sudden end by falling into Boardman's 60ft. It was a clay hole, and used belong to the Albion, they had a yard down there, agen the Pit. We used to go there tiddlerin'. We spent no end of time round there.'

wrong minute you could be in trouble. There were holes at the side of the railway, and when a shout went up you knew the cable had snapped, and everybody kept out the way, and it just landed in a pile.

I knocked myself out once, I was carrying two - twelve inch pipes on my shoulder, and I was crossing this railway line, and there was puddles of water, and I stepped in the wrong puddle, and it was a hole. I fell down, and this twelve inch pipe hit my head against a rail. It knocked me out. They took me down to Burton Hospital, the one in New Street, for an X-ray, but I was alright. I've caught meself many a time.

When the pipes were stacked in the yard, the little uns were stacked up nicely, but you had a row of twelve inch pipes on the ground, and then they rolled the next lot up a plank, and along that, planks to the end, and as you went higher, you'd have to shove another plank up, and in the winter time, the chances of 'em slipping back off the plank was enormous.

There was one man who used to do the gullying. He used to do the pipes, conduits for cables, and this bloke worked on a section there, and they had to put black sort of pitch tar on the tops, and he always walked across the yard, and his raincoat was down to his ankles, and he carried a bucket of fire in both hands, taking it across the yard. We often said to him, "You'll go on fire one day," and he always said, "Oh no," but one day, he did catch fire, well his coat was all greasy and oily, you see. They got some blankets and wrapped him up and took him to first aid. He eventually recovered.

I earned about £8 - £12 a week, and one day the foreman said "Would you like some overtime?" We said, "What doin'?" and he says, "Fillin' bags of slack," and we said, "Oh arr," so me brother and me, we stopped Saturday afternoon, about four hours, or something, and we said to each other, "We'll have a bit in our pay packet at the end of the week," but we only got 6d, that's 2½p for four hours.

So, when the foreman says, "How are you fixed for next week," I said "No thanks, you can keep it." When I left, and went to Pirelli, I realised I'd been killing meself at Wraggs it was such hard work.

If you didn't carry the pipe properly and put a dent in it, you had a scuff at the back of the ears, 'cause you'd have ruined it. At the end of a week, on a Friday, you didn't get your money from the office. The fettler would keep it. He had a contract and whatever he made, he gave you what he wanted and that was your employment. I wasn't satisfied with that so I went into what they called the opening hole. That's where they got the clay and men used to fill the clay by shovel into tubs. We used to clip these tubs with metal clips onto an endless haulage, which used to take them up to what they called the pug, to be ground up and we had to fill these tubs and send them up in sequence. There was yellow, brown, pink and whatever they were making you had to send them, so that when they were tipped into the pug, they were mixed.

I worked at the Albion Clay Company, Woodville which made large pipes up to 2¼ hundred weight. Youngsters like myself worked on machines making two, three, four and five inch sewage pipes. It was contract work. If you managed to do your count every day, without any problems like waiting for clay because it was raining, you might be lucky and earn around £3 a week.

It cost four pence half penny (4½d) return from Ashby to Woodville on the Midland Red Bus and many times I and others have trudged through huge snowdrifts to get to work when the boundary road was blocked. No work, no pay those days.

There were two fellows making bricks by hand and meself and another boy had to carry them on two pieces of wood when they'd made them and place 'em on the floor to dry. The next day, you had to turn them over before you started making them again. If they'd dried too quick or there was anything wrong with the clay and there was a slight crack in it, it was thrown out. But as you went and put these bricks on the floor, there was an actual fire under the floor and you had blisters galore, even if you wore clogs to try and resist the heat.

I can remember women who were working in the pipe yard, going out in the avenues where I lived at Midway. They would be wearing headscarves to cover their rollers because they were p'r'aps going out that night to the Rink, or even catching a train to Blackpool to the Tower Ballroom, and then catch another back and arrive about 2 o'clock in the morning.

I sometimes lay in bed at Midway and I could hear the Blackpool train making its way up to Woodville from Swad, and they would have to double head it. They'd have to hitch another engine on to it, to get it up the incline to Woodville. You could hear this thing thrashing. It would be 1 o'clock, 2 o'clock in the morning. You'd hear the wheels spinning, skidding on the lines as it tried to get up the incline to Woodville, two engines on it.

I heard a story about one lady in particular, I won't mention any names, but I understand she was quite a well built lady, and since the kilns and feeding the kilns and drawing the kilns, was a very hot job and very heavy work. It was said that she thought nothing of stripping off to the waist, and working in that environment like that, and sometimes in the winter she might just wrap an overcoat round her, and that was it.

Women went out to service,
There was typing for one or two,
And in the pot banks and the pipe yards
They had manual work to do.
Swad folk were known for labour
For digging, carting and graft
But did they get enough credit
for their artistry and craft?

I was fifteen when I went to Greens, and jobs were very scarce really. You'd either got to go into Service or work for people. If you were clever enough, you could be a typist but there wasn't anything round here much for us except Greens or somewhere like that. Neither Mum or Dad wanted me to go, but we had a friend that had worked there for years, and she said I would be all right at the job that she got for me, and she'd take care of me, so that was why I went.

There was no buses before 6 o'clock in the morning and often three times a week, say Monday, Wednesday, Friday, we would have to be there for 6 o'clock in a morning and the buses didn't start that early. I lived at Linton then and I'd have to walk from there to Greens, which was quite a long way to get there for 6 o'clock, to do this drawing as they call it. The kilns if I remember rightly, had got to start at the bottom, and they'd go through the different floors and right into the sky almost.

It was very hard work, I'll tell you. Most of the men drank the previous night, I'm not saying at work, because they weren't allowed to do that. But oh dear, the sweating - because the kilns were so hot. It was terrible. The smell of drink and onions! Anyway, we got by all right.

It was in the warehouse where I used do a lot of work. When the pots came out of the kiln they'd got silica sand inside, which had to be brushed out. The brush was quite crude really. Lots of bristles in, fine bristles, and we used to have to sweep it out. It

In this one room, we had to sort the best out. They had to be special for the best. There'd be seconds too but if anything wasn't good enough we used have to get all that gathered together so that it could be ground up again and used for other things. There used to be these shutters as opened and underneath there'd be a cart. We had to throw this rubbish as they called it, into this cart to be taken away.

didn't seem to do us any harm, but don't think it did us much good.

When you first start, you worry because you mustn't leave one little speck of sand in that bowl or else it would make a hole when it was dipped in the glaze. But as we got more used to doing it we could do it in four goes. You go 'one, two, three, four,' and all the sand would be gone.

Then we had a little conveyance that was in the warehouse. There was one wheel at the front, like a big barrow, and two wheels at the back, and they used to be p'r'aps four of us with this conveyance and sometimes the floor of the next bit was lower, and it had got a little bit just about big enough for this to go by. Once it slipped off the side, and it's a wonder I didn't break me foot when the wheel dropped on it. Of course, I had to go down to the bottom bank, see the manager, and such like, and I still remember to this day him saying to me, "Mary, Mary quite contrary, how does your garden grow? You was a silly girl wasn't you!" I've remembered it to this day. I was only off work about a fortnight to three weeks. But it really killed me, and it was very painful. It still hurts today.

When the ware was in this biscuit stage and you were doing this brushing out, your finger ends used to get raw, absolutely raw with the roughness. We had lots of trouble keeping them right, we used have to cream them and do. They used say you've got to put 'em in the chamber pot. It was the salts whatever that did it. But we had some nasty fingers through that. We didn't even have anything protective on the end of our fingers.

On the ground level I would say it was like a furnace, and we'd stand round the kilns at various intervals and there would be like a rough slab on either side. At the top would be two slabs. We had these earthenware dishes and put whatever we wanted to cook in it. Bacon, sausage or anything, put it all in and it would cook lovely on top of these slabs. We used have a hot dinner. We used do tomatoes and all sorts of things, and it used be lovely, but that wasn't everyday, you used tek your ordinary lunch the other days, but they didn't mind us doing that and there was this little pub down below (It's still there I think) where we could go and buy a lot of the stuff that we needed, because I always used to buy the sauce for one thing; HP sauce, and I can remember it was surprising how many came to fetch this bottle. It didn't last long.

Two recent pictures on Mary's wall
Delicate, sensitive paintings of flowers
Were there in her fingers through all those hours
She worked on the pot bank and emptied the kilns.
But pictures of a different kind
Held like magic in a silver beam
Sprinkled people's work-worn lives
With stars, adventure and the chance to dream.

chapter four

Entertainment

Shall we dance?

Life seemed far more romantic than it is today
at dances.
You could forget the real world for a while
as people do
watching television now
or reading Mills and Boon.
The young men would come over and ask:
"May I have the pleasure?"
and take us back to our seats
afterwards.

We wore lovely long slinky dresses
and changed into dainty shoes
out of respect
for the polished floor.

Ernie always wore patent leather
dance shoes.

I wonder if there are many people who can remember
the Rink dances now?
The waltzes,
slow fox-trots that needed
perfect balance,
the barn dance,
Valetta,
'excuse me,'
Paul Jones dances
and spotlight prizes?

Ernie always wore evening dress
and looked smart.

One day, in the middle of May, 1991 I was feeling in a mood to reminisce about those days not so long ago. I decided to go and see what the old dance hall, the Rink was being used for in the 90's.

It was a hot day, and against all common sense, I began to walk, knowing full well it would take me at least an hour to get there. Now, the Rink, it's hard to describe it in words but the Rink was loved by everybody, not only in this particular area in Swadlincote, but people came from miles around to dance there, because it was just an incredible thing. I had my camera with me, hoping to take a few shots of the old place, not that the building was anything to look at, it wasn't, but it held such a special place in my heart, for I had spent so many happy hours there.

It had been years since I had walked through the Alexandra Rink passage that led to the famous dance hall in Swadlincote and, as I reached the building, the scene that confronted me was so bad, I felt devastated. The windows were boarded up, and there was graffiti all over the walls. It was obvious that it hadn't been used for anything in a long time. I walked all round the building, but there was no sign of life; all was still. I leaned against the railings for a while and thought to myself, "How sad," and I carefully put my camera away, unused.

There was no-one else around, so I stood there and allowed my mind to go back to the 1950s and using the power of my imagination I gradually heard drifting faintly on the breeze, the sound of imaginary voices, and I pretended it was Wednesday, because that was the day of the week that the big bands used to come, and in my mind's eye, I could see the crowded dance floor, full of happy faces, enjoying every moment. Joe Loss was playing his signature tune - *In the Mood.* They would be dancing a quickstep.

He then began to slow the tempo down by playing a slow foxtrot, followed by a modern waltz. His lead singer, Rose Brennan, took the limelight. She was a good singer and each dancer felt that her smile was for them alone. She deserved the ovation given to her, as with a final wave of the hand she finished the melody and sat down.

The dancing went on through the repertoire of the band. Not only modern ballroom dancing, but old time favourites like the barn dance and then on to the more exotic dances, the samba, rumba and the cha cha cha.

Just when the dancers were about to drop with exhaustion, it was the drummer's spot. The dancing stopped, as it always did, and throngs of appreciative dancers stood around the bandstand, enthralled by the drum solo. He finished with a mighty clash of his symbols, and the clapping began, and seemed to go on forever. The dancers then

On the outside it looked like a corrugated sheeted building did the Rink. But inside, the floor was immaculate. It was filled with a myriad of beautiful lights, all shining on the slatted floor. Just wonderful.

returned to the floor, refreshed, and after a few more dances the band began to play *The Last Waltz...*

Hair set, seams straight, ready to go
And your heart beat skips to a strict tempo
Saturday night to the Rink for the dance
Hoping for a quick step to romance
Glamorous nights, dancing years
Happy hours, memories, one or two tears.

When I first went there, that Saturday night, I went with a friend. Got on the bus. We weren't wearing long dresses that particular day because it was Saturday, and the big dances were on a Wednesday, where such as Joe Loss came, and Victor Sylvester, oh and a lot of others, too many to name.

We walked up the Rink passage. As we did, you could hear the music in the background and your adrenaline began to run you know, as you came up the passage, and you began to get excited. 'Oh, What's it gonna be like? Will there be many there? Will there be anyone I know?' and we got up to the top, to the door, and there's a queue, because everybody wanted to go there, and we went in and it wasn't very much - only about a shilling, maybe one and sixpence, and we went in and stood there.

The band was so loud in your ear, it absolutely blasted out and we looked round both of us did, and my friend Valerie, she looked at me and said, "Cor, isn't it beautiful, just look at that floor," and it shone so much. I've never seen a floor shine so much as that, and then we went to the cloakroom, which was on the left, and there were two ladies there taking your shoes. "Give us your shoes," she'd say, "and your coats," and then she'd hang them up, and give us a ticket, you see. "Now don't lose your ticket," she'd say, "or you won't get your clothes back."

So then we asked, "Where do we go now?" and she pointed to where the ladies room was, which was right over the other side. So we had to walk all the way round. It was like, there were seats all the way round, and then like a little corridor went all the way round as well, so you could walk wherever you wanted to go, outside the dance part.

We went to this door, and opened it, and heard the noise of the girls laughing and talking. We went in there, and it was just an empty room, except for clothes everywhere. There were even coats in there as well, so some didn't take their clothes to the cloakroom, but what amazed me, was this great big long mirror, which was all the way along the room on one side, and there was a shelf underneath it, and there was all makeup bags, everything to do with makeup all the way along, you know, and we looked and exclaimed, "Good grief!"

So we powdered our noses again, and put extra lipstick on, and then got the old perfume out - the *California Poppy* perfume or *Evening in Paris*. I had *Evening in Paris*, and then when we'd sort of finished taking off the shiny noses, and making sure we were all right, you know, titivating the hair and everything, we put our makeup bags on the shelf, that's what we did, in a certain spot, right on the end, 'cause I thought, 'I'll never find mine in the middle, never, and then we sort of took a deep breath, opened the door and out we went.

There we were in this corridor part with all these boys and girls milling round, and young men, and so Valerie looked at me, and she said "What if nobody asks us to come and dance," she says, "I'll feel such a clot!" and I said, "Don't worry, someone is bound to come and ask us."

So we sort of crept on to the dance floor itself, and sat down in this seat together, you know, shaking. Couldn't help it, and then all of a sudden, this young man came up, and he stood in front of me and he says, "Could I have the pleasure of this dance please," and I thought, 'I know him, I've seen him before somewhere' and I thought, 'Yes, he works at the same place as I worked at,' so I thought, 'That's good, I'll dance with him, it's nice to have someone you know,' and I thought, 'Oh dear, what about Valerie,' leaving her there. I didn't like to leave her there, but by then somebody had walked up to Valerie and asked her to dance, and there we were on this floor. This very shiny floor.

I put my arm on his shoulder, and he put his round my waist, and then we began. It was a quickstep I remember and I'd learned how to do a quickstep, so there I was tripping the light fantastic on the most famous dance floor in the Midlands.

The thing is, he knew more than I did. He knew all the twists and turns. He used to call them telequick, twinkle, or something like that. We danced around the room, and he was such a good dancer and it was like floating. It really was like floating, and you felt as though, well, you just felt lifted somehow. It must have been all the adrenaline. We floated round the room, two or three times, then he took me back to my seat, and we sat down. But I had lots of dances with him, and he became a full-time partner, and I ended up marrying him as well!

Ernie Hall, dancing master,
Dapper and debonaire,
Glided as if on castors,
Always had a red rose to wear.

Ernie would shuffle round the floor, keeping his eye on people. He never really let his end slip sort of thing. He looked the part and you had no need to ask who the manager was when you went in there. Ernie looked that all the time. He would never allow jitterbugging on the floor - which was a dance the Yanks brought over. If he saw someone in a corner, you know, doing a bit, he would soon move them on. "None of that here. Else you're out!" he'd say.

He always had a couple of bouncers on the door. They weren't like the bouncers you get today, but there'd be a couple of them ready to put anybody out that was acting awkward. There was the odd argument at one time but it used to get sorted out pretty quickly. None of this kicking one another's heads in, as some seem to do now."

There were lots of bands that came to the Rink, but Victor Sylvester was my favourite. He came in 1956 and we had to dance our best for him, and we had to have a long dress because we had to look real posh.

On Saturday nights we went to the Hop, it only cost just over a shilling (5p) but the big bands used to come in the middle of the week, on the Wednesday. I can remember when Eric Delaney came, and Edmundo Ross, Marion Ryan was his singer, but you forgot the names over the time.

I loved to dance, but I was disappointed when I discovered that Eric couldn't dance; we were going out at the time. He went for lessons at Burton, somewhere, but he only went twice, he's got two left feet, so I used to go without him.

Ernie Hall was a local character. He was a professional dancer and used to teach dancing. He always appeared as if he was going to a big do - something like a garden party at the palace. He would have his frock tail coat on with his shoes all black and immaculately polished and his dicky bow and cravat.

When I was young I lived with me dad and mam at Church Gresley and I used to go dancing at the Rink. I always walked back home with one of my friends and we used to pass me dad going to work at Gresley Pit. But on this particular night we were late coming home and I never passed him and thought, "I hope he hasn't gone yet," but he had.

When I got home I found that he'd locked the middle door and me mam had gone to bed. I had to sleep in the back kitchen under some old macs. It were about six o'clock in the morning when I woke up and I banged on the door so hard me mam thought we'd got burglars. Anyway, she came running down and she said, "Who is it?" and I said, "It's me," and she let me in. I were ever so cold. It were in winter and when me dad got home from pit they had the biggest argument out.

It were lovely at the Rink. I had lots of partners to dance with and I met me husband George there. I used to go with his sister but I didn't know that he were her brother at the time. We got married and lived at Newhall, but he's been gone five years now, and I'm 80 this April.

My sisters and friends and I went to many of the Saturday evening dances and sometimes to Ernie's classes on a Tuesday. Occasionally, there were what we called the 'Big Dances' on Wednesday evenings. We walked there initially, because we couldn't afford to go on the bus. I was a student then and hadn't started work, so it meant a three-mile walk there and back. It seems strange now that we had no fears of the dark or of meeting any unsavoury characters, and we never did. We girls were very innocent and naive then compared with today's seemingly worldly-wise young. I'm not sure which is the better. I know I thoroughly enjoyed my youth, struggling for existence though we were.

At that time we only had one shilling (5p) a week pocket money and had three choices of how to spend it. The cinema, the dance, or stay at home and draw fashion pictures or try to write stories while we mugged ourselves with sixpenny worth (2p) of chocolate, and saved sixpence towards a new pair of shoes or clothing. Our choice varied but it was mostly the dance that won. If you learned until you were a good dancer, there was no difficulty in getting partners to dance all night long. What energy we had! Ernie could keep up with us too. Sometimes we had the rare privilege of dancing with him.

When we had the Paul Jones, you changed partners. I don't know why it was called that. It seemed to exist so that you could meet lots of people and it was good for the wallflowers. They also had a spotlight which added real glamour. Sometimes, you got a prize - chocolates or wine - if you were standing under the particular spot when the music stopped.

We'd wear walking shoes of course to get there and then you'd take them off once you got in. They would be something like black satin court shoes or shoes with little diamond studs or with straps round your ankles. They were always high heels, some wore three inch high heels and I don't know how they managed to dance in them but they were very, very glamorous. If you had a white dress, you'd have white satin shoes and red shoes to go with a red dress. It would all match. We'd spend our money on these things, especially when we started to work. If we wanted to go to the big dances, we sometimes sat up all night altering dresses, putting on frills and sewing them by hand. It used to take a long time, but we were dedicated because it was so different from our normal existence which was very hard.

Jiving and rock and roll are enjoyable but with them the courtesy of yesteryear has almost gone. We have to move on, of course, and live in the present, but I'm glad I was part of those lovely dancing years.

The evenings I had at the Rink left me with an enduring excitement for life. It's a feeling that I have with me now for everything. I never lose that pure feeling of being alive. Every day is wonderful to me. And I've still got that excitement, a little spark which I'm sure comes from those days. My eldest daughter is with the Derby Opera Company and she was saying the other day, "Mum, I always seem to have this little spark inside!" She's great fun to be with, always laughing. It's a wonderful thing to have really because you never grow tired and it doesn't matter if things go wrong - you've still got it inside.

If someone mentioned Monkey Parades to the youth of the 90s, they would ask - whatever's that? Well, when I was young I didn't know either.

In the 1930s my mum used to push my pram all the way from Hartshorne, to the middle Pit Row in Church Gresley, where my Gran lived. It was a distance of roughly four miles, and my mum would think nothing of walking along those narrow, unlit, uncrowded lanes. The only things that she passed would be a tractor, the odd fox or a pheasant flitting from one field to another.

As I grew old enough to make the same journey on foot, it became a regular thing to visit Gran. On the way back home, we'd cut through the passage that led into Swadlincote's High Street, and, if it was Sunday, I was amazed to see the street full of people, because the shops in those days never opened on Sunday, so when I asked Mum what the people were doing, all she said was - "You'll understand when you're grown up."

She was right. I was in my early teens before I got to know the answer. Apparently, it was a local custom, a way of socialising - where a boy gets to meet girl.

The idea was that, if a boy saw a girl he liked, perhaps at the place where he worked, he would go to Swadlincote on a Sunday evening, and walk *up* one side of the High Street, and then back *down* the other side, hoping that by chance he would see her there.

We were very naive in those days. You can tell that by what happened to these two young men. One said to the other, as they entered the High Street one Sunday evening, "Now what do we do, Tom?" "I'm not sure," said Tom. "I think that if we see a girl we like, we're supposed to grab her as she walks by." "Is that it then?" said his mate, Fred. "Yes, that's all I know," said Tom, and they began walking *up* the High Street. After a few minutes Fred nudged his mate, and pulled at his sleeve. "Look!" he said. "There's that girl I told you about at work." "Go on then," said Tom. "Grab her as she comes by," and that's just what Fred did, but to his horror, his advances were not returned, and the girl spun round and hit him with her handbag. He turned away, his ego deflated, and ran straight into a lamppost. Tom and Fred then made a hasty retreat into the nearest pub, and no doubt Fred hid his embarrassment behind a pint of Burton's best beer - well, it was only a few pence in those days.

As I walk through the town sometimes
The buildings seem to speak
And echoing ghostly voices seem to drift along the street.
Time and space are merging,
I can see it all once more,
All the friends I used to know
Are standing in the doors
I'm back there street parading
On a summer Sunday night
All the boys and girls are there
Much to my delight.

A mate of mine always said the palais glide got him married. They were doing the palais glide and this girl kept kicking him from behind, you know, he were in a row. He said, "Of course, eventually I married her.

I never had a girl friend from the Monkey Parades, but I did go Monkey Parading with my cronies. You had a Sunday Best as against your every day clothes. Invariably, it'd be long trousers and black shoes. Most people wore black shoes, white shirts, tie, jacket. Might have a button hole as well, depending on how you felt, and if you were one of the brave men who could afford to buy cigarettes, you might be swaggering along and having a puff of a Woodbine as well. Nothing happens like that now, and in a way it's sad really that things like this have gone.

There were no nylons then. Ladies wanted the artificial silk stockings. I'm saying straight after the war and they were only 5p a pair. If they couldn't afford them they would paint their legs to make sure they'd got a seam up, so they would paint their legs in a tan or a fawn, with a black line up, and you really thought they were stockings from a distance, but otherwise they would be quite smartly dressed. There were no anoraks, they'd probably be in a costume or a blouse and skirt, or jumper sort of thing.

When me and John were courting, we used to walk around Bretby and sometimes we'd stop at the top of Midway Road and call at the Mason's Arms for a packet of biscuits. They were tuppence a packet of four biscuits with cheese in and sometimes he would stand outside and look to see if there was anybody about we knew and I'd make haste in and fetch this packet of biscuits. There was no way we dare let anybody know we were going in a pub, not even for a packet of cheese biscuits.

Rock 'n' Roll and the Rink

Ernie Hall put a little rope
up in the corner saying
'If you want to jive
get over that rope
and that was the start of rock 'n' roll
Of course
Ernie realised after a while
that you'd never stop
rock 'n' roll
so what he did
eventually
was to get a dance band
and a rock group
so the evening was split
equal
and this pleased everyone.

I lost me Mum when I was nine and I was adopted by me Mum's sister. Now, as a teenager, they was in their late fifties, very old fashioned. And when we used to go monkey parading at Swad, we didn't let them know. We used to tell lies. So a friend of mine and myself we used to say we was going to the youth club at the chapel at the bottom of the road. At this youth club they'd play your records and you could have a dance.

Well, this particular night I forgot to take my records and off we went monkey parading. So when I came back, my uncle said, "Did they play any of your records tonight?" I said, "Yes." He said, "Now I know you're lying, I know you've not been to the youth club. Because I came down to bring the records to you. And you wasn't there."

He was a friend of my friend's dad, they worked together in a pipeworks, at Church Gresley. They got to know that we went monkey parading, so they'd arranged to follow us. We was in the bus park, and was talking to all these lads, and we was deciding where we was going to go thinking perhaps of a walk through Swad or going to Swad Park. The next thing, my friend Mary's dad had got hold of the collar of *her* coat, my uncle had got hold of the collar of *my* coat and said, "The next place you're going is home!" Oh, we was so frightened! Anyroad, they stopped me from seeing the man who is my husband now, but, of course, we managed to get to see each other plenty of times despite that setback!

It was very lively in Swad, in the 60s. There was a lot of monkey parading and a lot of young girls and boys, down the bus park. You'd got the bus park café where a lot of them went in and the picture houses and the Rink. You know, there was plenty for us to do as teenagers.

If you was monkey parading on a Friday night you would probably have your curlers in because you was going to the Rink on the Saturday you see. And you used to have your curlers in all through the night, you slept in them, and put a nice head scarf on and tied in under your chin and round the back. So you went monkey parading in your curlers. Most of us did anyway. And it was just sort of, up and down the High Street, and the lads on one side and the girls on the other, you know. 'My mate fancies you.' And 'Will you go out with her?' And 'See you at the Rink on Saturday.' And that sort of thing.

The Milk Bar was a haven for local teenagers. In present day terms, it was just a coffee shop. You went through and there was a bar but if you walked down a passage, there was a small restaurant at the back where you could get a table. The owner installed what was the first juke box in the area. You'd never seen anything like it. You saw them in American films with their lights but to have one in Swad was quite something. The Milk Bar was *the* place to go.

My auntie worked there and would keep all the food waste in a separate dustbin at the back and my only encounter sadly with the excitement of the Milk Bar was with a wheelbarrow, every Saturday when I'd go and collect all the wastefood in sacks, for the pigs my dad kept. You didn't get commercial feed in those days. You fed them with what you could get.

In the fifties, the usual mode of dress for a young man going to the Rink for a night out was a sober two piece suit, collar and tie and leather shoes. The jacket was quite short

The police'd come along "Come on now, move on out this doorway". But I mean, you'd never dream of doing any damage. It used be packed, we didn't even go snogging 'cause we was all so innocent in those days. Happy days they were. You had fun without causing any trouble to anybody.

and the trouser bottoms wide. Some men would adopt a smart sports jacket and flannel trousers for a less formal effect.

A group of us, about a dozen, adopted the dress of what could be described as Pseudo-Edwardian. The main difference between a conventional suit and a 'Teddy' suit was that the latter jacket was a great deal longer, and the trousers narrower. Some men liked to wear the collar studded and cuffs finished in velvet. The favourite hairstyle was the DA, made popular by Tony Curtis. Sideburns were popular when Elvis Presley sported them in the Rock and Roll period. I had a good collection of the early songs recorded by Elvis Presley, Little Richard, Bill Haley and Jerry Lee Lewis. They were on the old 78 rpm, 12 inch shellac records, which were very easily broken. I used to buy two and break one which made if difficult and expensive to build up a collection.

Pubs with juke boxes were very popular with the young set. The first one I came across in our area, was at the Spread Eagle in Newhall. The machine contained a selection of about 30 records, and because they were 12 inch discs, when they were put on to play, they crashed down on to the turntable with a loud bang! To return to clothing, I bought my first suit from Harry Burnton who had a stall selling menswear under the Shambles. It was an ordinary charcoal grey garment, but modified by Harry who reduced the width of the trouser bottoms from 20 inches to 14 inches. With this I wore black shoes and white socks, and a white shirt with a Slim Jim tie.

Having acquired a taste for this style, I had a made to measure fawn gabardine suit from Blackburns in Burton. They were about the only national tailors who would fashion such an article. The jacket was fingertip length and fastened almost up to the neck with five buttons down the front.

My favourite and last 'Teddy' suit was made for me by a Birmingham tailor. The material was of dark but bright blue with green and white flecks. Under street lights it appeared to be purple and it was a striking colour and much admired by young men at pop concerts. I was going through my colourful period, as one can deduce, when my choice of accessories consisted of a yellow shirt, green suede crepe soled shoes, and a waistcoat in hunting pink. The jacket was of drape style, fingertip length and trousers 14 inches wide. One afternoon I was walking along the Main Street in Long Eaton when an elderly woman ran excitedly across the road with no thought for safety in her haste through the traffic. She grabbed me by my lapels and shouted, "You must be…colour blind!"

This suit was my pride and joy but I was refused admittance to many staid venues -

not the least being the Tower Ballroom in Blackpool, when on holiday. I gained admission later in the week by borrowing a jacket and trousers from a friend who was sharing the same digs. Unfortunately, he had very short legs. And so I had to wear the trousers very low round the waist, in order that the trouser bottoms were not 'half mast.' Because of this, the crotch was only just above the knee - sartorial elegance indeed.

You'd do a set of quicksteps. They'd usually play three of each dance and you'd then sit down and have a talk. They'd say, "Take your partners for a waltz," and they'd play three, same with the foxtrot and then they'd do an old time selection - barn dance, followed by a valletta, a St Bernard's Waltz, a military two step - then later on it'd be the palais glide, the okey cokey, the conga...lovely.

Couldn't wait to get there. All dolled up. Put the DA right. As you first went through the doors, the bandstand was to your right and to the left would be the buffet. There was no beer on the premises. The top originally was a snooker hall but they turned it into a cloak room. The floor itself had a rail around, where you could watch the dance or sit and drink your tea or coffee.

They used to have a globe for the smoochy dances. They'd throw a couple of spots on it and it'd send all these balls of light around the room. All the glitter from the dancers' shoes would shine and be reflected. 'Course I was turned down quite a few times. Sometimes you'd get to walk them home. Say they lived in Woodville (I lived in Newhall), you'd walk them to Woodville and walk all the way back. The main thing was to make sure they got back safely.

Dancing at the Rink in the 60s was Tuesday, Thursday and Saturday. One was live music, but other nights were records. These were the days of Rock 'n' Roll, pre-Beatles, and it was all this modern sort of standing about, shaking your arms around dancing, so there was lots of jiving.

There was a certain part of the evening that you weren't allowed to jive, and we all did the Palais Glide. The well-kept dance floor was famous, but I don't suppose my generation appreciated it: probably the previous generation did, because of the ballroom dancing, but there was *no* ballroom dancing in my day. However, The Rink was still *the* place to go, and it was always packed, except for the summer months. When the Beatles came along, the dance scene changed, and so did the music but it was still atmospheric.

First place we made for was the toilets to check that our hair was okay. Hair styles

were bouffant, or flicked up at the bottom or piled on top of your head in big curls. When we came out we'd get a drink - coke - then we'd walk round to eye up the talent. Lads weren't keen on getting up to dance, so we used to go up to them and say, "Oh come on, let's have you up for a dance," and they'd say, "Oh no!" so we'd say "Right, if you get up for a dance, you might get a date with a girl that you like," to bribe 'em basically into it. Once we got them on the dance floor, we had to keep our part of the bargain, and get them paired off with someone else, but that wasn't always successful.

If two girls were dancing together, the lads who were really good at jivin' would come across and dance with both of us. We had records like Elvis Presley - *Jailhouse Rock, Blue Suede Shoes* and *Rock Around the Clock*. Then there was Bill Haley singing. They were all good music for jiving.

The men of the area used to go the pub first, then on to the Rink later. The girls were always dancing hours before the men. They'd meet you there, well, that way they didn't have to pay for you to go in, you see. But that can't be just peculiar to South Derbyshire, I should think. I don't know, maybe it is! Oh yes, they'd all congregate in the pubs first, and you'd go up to the Rink with a girlfriend, and take it from there. They'd always meet you later when they'd had a few pints of ale.

Marlene 'Sentimentally Yours'. That was me in my early singing career. Taken in 1952, you see me at the Majestic. The stars on the curtain behind me were sewn on by a young man who later became my husband and much of our life together was spent in Swad's cinemas. Warwick was a projectionist, mainly at the Majestic but helped out at the Empire and I did many of the Sunday Shows. Despite the close proximity of these worlds it was two or three years until we met properly, eventually touring together with pantomimes and shows. I used to sneak upstairs to his projectionist box and we did all our courting there, in that box during the twenty minute film reels.

The best evening I remember was when Jack Parnell came and Phil Seaman came from Burton on Trent. They did a drum duet of a tune called *Skin Deep*. Jack was on the left hand side of the room and Phil was on the right and they did a duet that must have lasted twenty minutes. Everything Parnell did, Seaman did but better and louder. Parnell would have a go and Seaman would top that, doing it better and louder. The audience was deafening when they finished. It was electrifying. Absolutely brilliant.

The adult social evenings like the Midland Red dance at the Rink, were attended by people from miles around, the annual dance was the best dance of the year. A friendly rivalry between the sports teams from each depot hit the high spot at the annual field day when all the family could attend and take part. In 1959 I remember collecting eight prizes, either sports equipment or household goods, from Mrs Sinclair, the general manager's wife. I remember how embarrassed I was when she suggested I sit on the steps and wait for my next prize, instead of trying to wriggle my way through the crowd.

There were some wonderful characters who worked on the buses. I will not try to name all the people who watched over or spied on us as the Midland Red youngsters, as I would never forgive myself if I left anyone out. But we all knew we could go to any member of the Midland Red family and whatever our problem was, they would sort it out.

The only time I needed assistance from any of the 'Midland Road family' was the time I missed the last bus into the village after a night at the Rink. I was seventeen at that time, all long lacquered hair and even longer match stick legs. My friend and I had been talking to a young man she knew and his friend, a tall ginger haired fellow. We know we should have gone to the bus station early because our bus always filled up quickly as it was only a single decker: a double decker could not go under the railway bridge on the outskirts of our village. Anyway we were late and could not get on the bus, even though I went to the front of the queue and asked. The driver said to ask my friend with the car. He had obviously seen us talking to my mate's friend, to get us to the turn round at our village and he would not tell my mum that we had missed the bus. So we went back into town to find my mate's friend. The ginger haired driver said he would take us home if he could have 'the tall skinny one', me!

He got us into the village well before the bus of course, so we had time to sit and talk. My mate's friend walked her to her gate and I waited for the bus, to let them know I was safely home. The ginger haired fellow asked me to see him the following day and we arranged to meet against the shop where the bus turned round. When the bus arrived I thanked him for the lift and went to thank the bus crew for not telling Mum about the missing bus.

The next day I got cold feet about going out with a man with a car, so I made sure I was out of the village at the time of our date. But when I got home, an hour after that time, to my horror he was still there! Not only still in the village but in my house with my mum. It seems my sisters had seen him driving up and down the street and he had asked them if they knew where I lived, so they had taken him in to wait for me. To this day I don't know what they said to each other. A year later we were married in the chapel near the shop.

Special buses were run late at night. They didn't have taxis. If we missed the last bus home we walked, but never on our own, always in twos or threes. The men used to say, "All right, we'll walk you home," and when we came out, the main thing was the chip shop, we used have to try and find a chip shop open. Lush's in the High Street used to always be open so we all used to go down to the chip shop and then we used to tek a stroll home, but we all used to walk home together, we was in the same area, going the same way. It wasn't a matter of 'you walk with that boy, or you walk with that one,' we all walked as a gang and a crowd of us, and then it was like, if you dropped off first, we were all walking with one another to the very end.

We just wanted a good time, so we didn't really want anything serious. We'd just be good friends with them, and then we'd just walk one another home. But we knew full well like, that if we wanted to go another week, and we hadn't got anyone to go with, we could ring one of them up and say, "Are you going down to the Rink?" and we would go with them, because it wouldn't make any difference whether you were a boy friend or a girl friend.

If you go out now to a do, either a wedding or something like that, it isn't very often there's anyone that can actually get up to dance, and do a proper jive, which I think is a shame really, because at the end of the day, there's some very good movements with the jive as well. You know very technical movements and completely different to what you see in the discos nowadays. The atmosphere of the Rink started to change as the bands faded away and the groups became the main attraction. It ended up as a bingo hall.

Skating, dancing, boxing, bingo, all went up in flames
But rake among the ashes and you'll turn up famous names
Who made their marks there,
wrote a page of their triumphant story
Newhall's Jack Bodell, who jabbed his way to glory
The British, Commonwealth and the European Crown
Lifted, brought home and paraded around the town.

I visited the Rink for the last time in June 1962 when a programme of professional boxing was put on. Top of the bill was Jack Bodell, having his sixth professional bout. His opponent was Roy Sewards of Lincoln, with the Midland light heavyweight title at stake. I was sitting on the front row and in the fifth round Jack lost his gum shield, not unusual for Jack, and it landed at my feet. I picked it up and took it back to Jack's corner, walking doubled up, a bit like Groucho Marx, so as not to spoil other people's view. When I returned to my seat, I looked up and the fight was over, Sewards having sustained an eye injury and so I missed the finish.

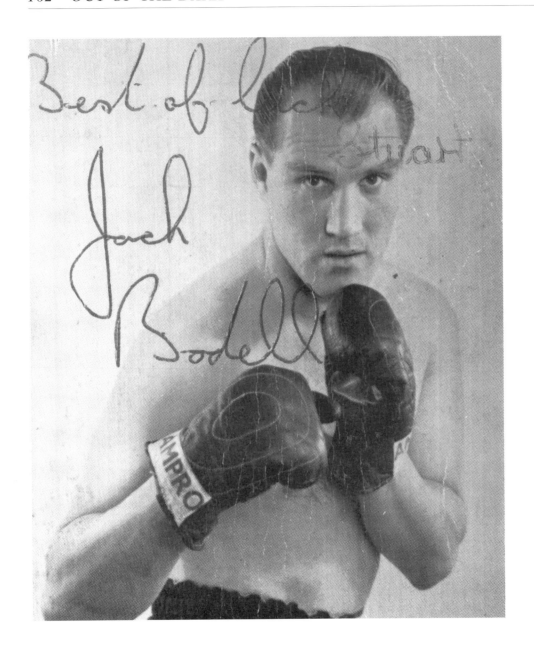

The outstanding sporting journalist of today, Hugh McIlveney had a book published of his best newspaper articles. In one of these pieces, he describes the shabby treatment meted out to Jack Bodell on his London appearances. For some reason, a section of the cockney crowd detested Swad born Bodell. The reminiscence I like best in the book is of McIlveney visiting Jack's dressing room after Jack had engaged in a gruelling fifteen round contest with Henry Cooper. Jack is demanding a drink, "'As anyone got any pop?" asks Jack. "There's a bottle of cola here, Jack," replies one of his entourage. "Hasn't anybody got any Swad pop?" responds Jack, "It's the best in the world!"

I saw Jack in Swadlincote High Street about a month ago and asked him if McIlveney's recollections were accurate. Jack replied, "Ay 'es rate theer!"

Jack Bodell first came to the attention of the sporting public in 1961 when he became British Amateur Light-Heavyweight Champion. In the final he put on a great performance, beating favourite Johnny Evans of Hammersmith on points. He also represented England at international level against the USA, winning the contest. Bodell turned professional in 1962, being guided by the uncle, Syd Bodell. He won his first five contests and on his sixth appearance beat Roy Seward to win the Midland area light-heavyweight title at Swadlincote Rink.

A disappointing 1964 ensued during which he had three fights, losing two, one being against the master boxer Joe Erskine, a former British champion. At this point Jack joined the stable of George Biddles, who managed him throughout the remainder of his career. In his first year under Biddles' wing Jack fought 16 times, winning 15. Winning ten out of 12 in 1966 and early 1967 he was matched with Henry Cooper for the British and Empire title. Jack made a promising start, winning the first round, but was beaten in the second when he fell foul of 'Enery's Hammer' as Cooper's left hook was called by his manager Jim Wicks.

It was back to the drawing board, but at the beginning of 1968 Jack had a very important win when he beat the personable Birmingham boxer Johnny Prescott. After victories in the same year over former British champion Brian London and Welshman Carl Gizzi, Biddles took a great gamble, jeopardising Jack's status as number one contender for another crack at Cooper by signing for a match with Billy Walker, the London Golden Boy known as the Blonde Bomber. Walker was very popular in London, his all action hard-hitting style going down well with fans. A sell-out at Wembley meant a big pay day for both boxers and so it proved.

Big John Robinson used to own the Rink and there'd be one or two troublemakers, and as soon as they came in and caused any trouble, John would get them by the scruff of the neck, and we stood and watched him you know. We used to love to watch him carrying them out. Out they went.

The fight was one of the most thrilling ever seen in this country. Jack started like a train and had Walker down for a count of nine and on the verge of a knock-out in the first round. Walker suffered a further knockdown in round two and took a terrific pounding. But Billy survived and Walker was nothing if not one of the bravest pugilists to step into the ring. Jack gave him a terrible hammering before the referee stopped the contest in Jack's favour in round eight. Two more wins and Jack was ready to meet Cooper again. At this time, however, Cooper was trying to get a fight with Jimmy Ellis, the WBA Heavyweight Champion. The British Boxing Board informed Cooper that should he beat Ellis they would not recognise him as champion since they only accepted WBC champions.

In a fit of pique Cooper relinquished the British title but the Ellis fight never took place. Jack was matched with his old opponent Carl Gizzi for the vacant belt. They met at Nottingham Ice Rink in October 1969 and Jack won a closely contested decision over 15 rounds. Bodell was British champion, the first southpaw to win this title.

Everything was now set up for a second contest between him and Cooper and this was arranged for March 1970. Once again Wembley Stadium was sold out. Cooper was an overwhelming favourite to win and it must be admitted that on this side of the Atlantic he was an outstanding boxer. The Cooper camp then indulged in what I can only describe as gamesmanship of the worst kind. Instead of Cooper following Jack into the ring straight away, he kept Jack waiting for more than five minutes in a darkened ring suffering all the agonies of a man with tremendous amounts of adrenaline running through him as is normal in this situation. Cooper won on points but it was a close contest.

Once again, having lost his title, Jack had to start again. He was now approaching 30 and time was running out. Four months after the Cooper fight Jack flew to South Africa and defeated their highly regarded boxer Jimmy Richards on points.

George Biddles wanted to keep Jack busy and arranged a match for him with the Mexican fighter Manuel Ramos who had met some of the best men in the world. The fight was staged at Wolverhampton Civic Hall. When the referee awarded Jack the decision, it was discovered that Jack had not lost a round.

A fortnight later he was back in the ring facing the dangerous Canadian Bill Drover. Drover had boxed Bugner to draw in what was supposed to be a warm up fight before he met Cooper. Jack came through the fight unscathed, winning a hard fight on points.

When we were courting we walked mostly, just looking at the stars. In those days you could see the skies was full of stars at night. You can't seem 'em now, because of the light and all the things swirling around in the atmosphere. You can only see one or two bright stars on a good night. We used to see everything - with me pointing out the Milky Way, and the Plough and the North Star to my girl friend - who ended up being my wife. We used to really enjoy ourselves, but we always had to watch the time. We had to be in by nine o'clock.

Jack then met Joe Bugner at Wembley for the British and Commonwealth titles. Bugner had just beaten the German Jurgan Buin to add the European crown to his laurels. The ballyhoo surrounding the Bugner fight was tremendous. For weeks it dominated the sports pages of the daily papers and the training quarters at the Royal Oak was inundated with reporters. Desmond Hackett, sports columnist for the *Daily Express*, promised to come to Newhall and clean Jack's bungalow windows in Rose Valley should he win. Many fans travelled to Wembley from South Derbyshire to witness their hero in action against a man who some judges tipped as a future world champion. When the decision was announced the referee's scorecard indicated that Jack had won 14 of the 15 rounds, one of the most one-sided championship bouts for many years.

On his return to Swadlincote Jack was given a Civic Reception and in a thank you speech delivered on the Town Hall steps he stated that, and here I paraphrase, there was more grit in the belly of one Swadlincote man than all the Londoners put together.

Now the holder of three major titles, the world seemed to be his oyster. Desmond Hackett duly came and cleaned his windows and the trade paper *Boxing News* ranked him eighth in the world.

Such is the fluctuating nature of boxing that Jack did not win another fight after that. His next outing was against the formidable American Jerry Quarry who carried too much fire power for Jack and defeated him in the first round. He quickly lost his European title to Jose Urtain, in Spain and at his last contest at Villa Park he suffered a humiliating defeat, losing his other titles to Danny McAlinden.

When Mohammed Ali was preparing for his world title defence against the German Southpaw Karl Mildenberger, he requested that Jack should help him prepare for the contest. So Jack had sparred with the legend. Yes, Jack Bodell certainly put Swadlincote on the map.

Swad's silver screens

At the Rink there used to be
what they called the "Tuppeny Rush"
or "Penny Rush"
we saved our pennies to go there
and each week
serials came on
and the hero
or heroine
would be left hanging
on a cliff
with her fingernails ready to drop off
or in a cellar full of water
up to their chins
and then the serial would end
and we were left in absolute
amazement
wondering how we would
get our penny again
next week
to go and see what happened.
Somehow the next week
the heroine or hero
always escaped
and to save the penny bus fare
back home to Linton
we would pretend we were
"Tom Mix" or "Buck Jones"
slappin' our behinds and galloping home
firing with two fingers
at anybody
who was going by.

If I was lucky enough to get what was called the Friday's penny, and that was not every Friday by the way, I would stand in the huddle of children outside the old Rink Cinema until the doors were opened. Can you imagine a hundred children suddenly surging in a mass to get the best seats? When order of some kind had been restored, the doors were closed and we were treated to the *Skater's Waltz* and one other tune I cannot remember the name of. I think they only had two records, for those were the only two I ever heard. Then the limping man came up the side of the cinema. A hushed whisper in the hall, "he's coming," then he went outside and you would hear the muffled chuffing of the gas engine that supplied the electricity for the projectors. The lights were dimmed and we were away galloping across the prairie, facing hordes of Indians and shooting the baddies. You could always tell the baddies for they were always dressed in black clothes with black stetsons. Laurel and Hardy were in their heyday then and they still make me laugh today when they are on the television. Boris Karloff and Bella Lugosi were the horrors of that day and many a time when turning out of the Rink, even in broad daylight, the children would be looking fearfully over their shoulders and some would run all the way home until they were safe indoors.

My late father, Mr Thomas Henry Taylor, otherwise known as Mr Harry Taylor, was projectionist at the Rink Cinema. My father's wages, before the Second World War, were only about £2.15 shillings. Eventually, he got between £5 and £6. My mother cleaned the Rink cinema and Empire for 10/- shillings a week and I used to help my father in the projection box.

I used to help my dad, by carrying the huge reels of film, all eleven hundred feet long: they were very heavy and I was only a school boy at the time. I used to rewind the films back onto empty reels, so that the films were the right way round for the next showing of the films and if I found a piece of film to be damaged, such as a sprocket hole broken, I had to tell my dad, so that he could then cut a frame, that is one picture, out of the film and fix it together again with acetate film fixing fluid cement. It was dangerous stuff to use, very inflammable and also poisonous. He used a small thin special brush to stick it to the film; there were 16 frames all the same, on the film, which went at 16 frames per second. To stop the jerking projection of the film on the screen, there was a device in the gate of each projector called a Maltese Cross, shaped like the German Iron Cross, which spun round at very high speed, in front of the film, as it passed through the projector gate.

Cinema films are loaded into the cinema projectors upside down and the Prizums lenses in the projectors then convert the pictures the right way up. Sometimes if we had someone fairly new to the job come to help my dad, they'd make a mistake, and project the film upside down. The audience in the cinema would whistle and shout, causing a disturbance till my dad stopped the film and put it the right way up. We had a paraffin oil combustion engine and dynamo generator producing the electric at the Rink Cinema. If that engine stopped, as it did on occasions, then the films stopped as well. At the new Empire Cinema when it was first opened, we had an old Rolls Royce aeroplane engine and dynamo generator till proper electricity was installed. When the Second World War started some officials and engineers from the Ministry of Defence came and took our aeroplane engine away for the war.

My dad projected the first full length sound film which was Al Jolson in *The Jazz Singer* in about 1928. The film was actually made in 1927. The sound of Al Jolson singing and talking was on a large 24 inch wax records (like the old 78rpm records used to be). Each reel of film had a record soundtrack to synchronise with the film and my dad timed the sound records with the films with the aid of an ordinary household alarm clock that he borrowed from my mother. When he had the silent films, there was a small band of about three or four local musicians who played music to the films. A lady named Nellie played the piano, a local watch repairer played the fiddle, and another man played either a cello or woodwind instrument.

My dad was a projectionist for near on fifty years. The last short while before he retired, he did the work of a Commissioner in a smart uniform standing at the doors of the Empire Cinema - that was at the end of World War two. The only memorabilia I have from the old Rink Cinema is a lens out of one of the silent projectors. It was given to my dad when the engineers came to dismantle the old projectors to replace them with new ones for better sound films.

Edwin Lawrence who lived in Weston Street, Swad and Tommy Rainer, who used to be in Sanger's Circus, set up a small film making company called the Albion Film Company and made three films. One was a 1913 *Parade*, the other a comedy called *The Plumber and the Lunatics* made around Swadlincote and the third was *A Noble Brother*, also made in Swad. In the film, Edwin needed a poacher and so our local hero, Charlie Hextall, who was well known for supplying rabbits and fish - nobody ever really asked where they came from - became a film star. When these films were shown at the Rink,

they played to packed houses and I think it was only the coming of the First World War that stopped it flourishing. Who knows, Swadlincote might have become another Pinewood Studios!

> **For years there were two cinemas**
> **And you could take your pick**
> **The Empire, rough and ready**
> **Or the grand Majestic.**

In my days the Majestic and the Empire were owned by the same people. The Empire didn't hold as many. It was built between the street and backing up to the clay works at the back, so because of the narrow plot it was built on, they tended to build it higher rather than longer and the big fault with it as a result was that if you were sitting in the balcony, you were looking right down at the screen. I remember in order to get the focus right on the projector, the screen was tilted back at quite an angle. If you had to sit on the front row, you'd be sitting like *that* and everybody was stretched out sideways on the screen. The Empire, being so much smaller and more compact didn't have the atmosphere of the Majestic.

When you went in the Majestic you were entering another world. For a start, it had its own grounds, and carpark. There was a sweetshop next door where you could buy sweets for the performance. The moment you went in, you went into a huge foyer with two staircases sweeping up like in *Gone with the Wind*. You had a much better view of the films because there was a big stage with the screen set back so that even if you were at the end of a row, you still had a good view. It had double seats upstairs, and in the interval between the films, we were entertained by Edwin Furness, who played the organ as it rose up smoothly through the floor, while girls came down the aisles selling sweets, chocolates and ice cream.

One of Swadlincote's most famous sons was part of this cinema world for a time. John Avery was a local boy, and to begin with, early in his career he was a projectionist at the Ritz in Burton, then he became the manager of the Majestic Cinema in Swadlincote, and was there for eight years. He also managed the New Empire after Mrs Hingley, and for those who remember, John's parents kept the Bear Inn, at which many of the top acts for the Majestic shows would stay.

Later, John moved to the Winter Gardens Circus at Skegness, followed by theatres general manager and a director of Stoll Moss Theatres. He joined the company as

At the Old Empire, you got your tickets, and there was a flight of steps each side. Mrs Gladys Winkle was the cashier then. When I was small, they didn't have tickets, they had a kind of metal thing cut out, and all different prices, and you had to give them back when you went through the door.

manager of the London Palladium, and was there fifteen years. Although he had the responsibility of eleven other theatres, the Palladium remained his favourite.

In 1955, when ITV launched Sunday Night at the Palladium, we saw again, the stars who had trod the boards here at the Majestic, in Swadlincote, and those who knew John often caught a glimpse of him as he stood outside the Palladium to greet the Queen and other Royals.

The Alexandra Palace of Varieties which was going in 1913 replaced the wooden Hippodrome.

Then a new Empire Theatre was built in West Street and opened on Boxing Day, 1912. Mr. Charles McCann of Derby was the main share-holder and the family, including Percy, moved to Swadlincote. This Empire was demolished in 1929-1930 and again a new Empire rose from the ashes. It was this Empire with which I became associated.

In the early days Mr. Walter Smith of Swadlincote was the projectionist, aided by Mr. Harry Taylor, who was a very pleasant person and could adapt to almost anything in the cinema line, doorman, newsboy for the Majestic and projectionist. Percy McCann was the manager of the Empire Cinema and New Majestic. Mr. Jim Smith, son of Walter, followed in his father's footsteps and became a projectionist at the Empire.

Sometimes, the cinematograph used to break down and the lads used to be wolf whistling and I think it was Percy McCann who used to come round with a torch threatening to turn them out.

In those days we used to wear hats, and once I had a hat on with a wide brim, and some lads behind me were throwing orange peel into it (fancy me having a hat on in the pictures). It just goes to show how foolish we can be when we're young.

We used to pay for the cheapest seats at the cinema which were right at the front, but you used to get a crick in your neck looking up at the screen, so when the usherette wasn't looking we used to shoot to the ones at the back and watch it properly. With what we saved, we used to buy sweets and ice cream.

The front seats were not too comfortable - the fire doors were on each side and often they would be partly opened by boys who tried to get in without a ticket. Middle and back seats were plush covered and tipped up, you had to hold it down with one hand and sit down before it tipped up again. Back seats were worth the bit extra. Couples preferred these as they could hold hands with no-one to watch.

Weekly miners' matinees

Courtesy Percy McCann
Who ran both picture palaces
Till a rising star began
To make his name
From small town cinema
To capital city fame.
Swadlincote's John Avery
Elegant in evening suits
From the Majestic to the London Palladium
Never forgot his roots.

Once John had got his feet under as manager, he introduced the well loved Sunday Shows. He saw the potential of the Majestic for entertainment, what with its dressing rooms and stage. We didn't have cinema performances on Sundays and John introduced live performances onto the stage. Up till then, there would only be two or three concerts a year and the pantomime. He started organising local talent shows and he had developed good contacts in London for popular top acts too. On some occasions, he himself would perform. I remember him miming the words to *Annie Get Your Gun* with someone from Hartshorne. John and this girl rehearsed and rehearsed and when they got on stage, people loved it. He was always so smart, welcoming guests in the foyer, but to see him on stage, dressed up and doing this comedy thing with somebody was a real eye-opener. He was a good sport and a real showman.

Besides films, we also had pantomimes and shows. Top stars would often be on the bill and there would be local acts and singers too. One memory of a dear friend Keith Fearn, when they had shows at the Majestic, compered by Barry Woods.

We were there one night, Keith and I, sitting on the front row and there was a hypnotist on stage and he invited the audience to clasp their hands above their heads. "But," he warned, "There might be some of you who will not be able to put your hands down again!" Without thinking, Keith clasped his hands tightly over his head and sat there grinning at me. "Now, those of you who can, release your hands," said the hypnotist. I looked at Keith and he seemed to be struggling with himself. "Put your hands down, Keith!" I said, "Stop fooling about!" "I can't!" he replied, laughing, "They're stuck!"

The hypnotist looked at the audience, "Would all those who can't release their hands like to come up on stage." Well, Keith had another go at trying to take his hands down but no matter how hard he tried, he couldn't. "I'll have to go up," he said, "I can't go home like this!"

Well, I really thought he was acting but he wasn't and he joined about ten others on stage who by that stage were sitting on imaginary hot seats and jumping all over the place. But halfway through the performance, Keith winked at me and I knew he was no longer under the hypnotist's influence but he still carried on doing the same as the others, which brought roars of laughter from the audience. When he finally returned to his seat, with his hands down, I whispered, "I knew you'd come out of it, but why did you carry on?" "Well, I didn't like to let the hypnotist down," he said, and that was the essence of Keith.

I was 13 when I became a projectionist; I was still at school at the time. That was in 1949, I started as a rewind boy at the Empire Cinema. My job was to rewind the films and check to see if there were any faulty joints. If there was I had to remake 'em ready for going on the projector to be shown.

Sometimes we had a special piece of film that was shared between the Empire and the Majestic, and if it went on at half-past-six at the Empire and was due at quarter-to-seven at the Majestic, I had to rewind it fast, check it for joints, run around to the Majestic, show it, and get it to come off, rewind it again and bring it back to the Empire. The job was quite active really.

I got into a bit of trouble at school being a rewind boy, they found out I was working and they had me on the carpet, but I ignored it and continued to work. Then when I was fifteen I left school. I dropped in for third projectionist place because the chief projectionist at that time, Dennis Stevenson, moved up to Leeds. A gentleman called Bill Swain went to chief projectionist.

John Avery was manager at the Empire and Majestic when I was there, he managed them both at the same time. He was only in his early 20s, he always looked very smart and was a real nice person to work for, a caring man who was interested in presenting the cinemas at their best. I can remember Edwin Furniss, the organist working at the Majestic, he used to come through the floor sitting on the organ playing his special tune. He also played during the interval.

I've got an old 78 record dated from 1950 and it's called *Let's Go To the Pictures*. It's by

Sometimes, the cinematograph used to break down and the lads used to be wolf whistling and I think it was Percy McCann who used to come round with a torch threatening to turn them out.

In those days we used to wear hats, and once I had a hat on with a wide brim, and some lads behind me were throwing orange peel into it (fancy me having a hat on in the pictures) it just goes to show how foolish we can be when we're young.

Phillip Green and his band. We used this record when we had to have advertisements. We used to play this record while the silent adverts were on, then following this came the main feature.

The words of *Let's Go To the Pictures* are as follows:

Let's go to the pictures
- to a picture show
Let's go to the pictures
- where the lights are down low.
Don't really care whether skies are grey or fine
'Cause we'll be holding hands together in a wonderland
where stars are always shin-ing.

Let's go to the pictures
- where we'll sit and dream
Two tickets to heaven
- on a silvery screen
We can ride the range west. Be a movie star's guest
Or a Juliet and Romeo
Let's go to the pictures
- to a picture show.

The record, when played, made everybody aware that the big picture was following that piece of music.

On Tuesdays there was an afternoon or morning performance for the miners of South Derbyshire. It was known as the Miners' Matinee. They used to argue about paying for a ticket, thinking that if they were unemployed, they could get in the cinema free. Many were the arguments I was involved in. Ordinary prices were 9d, 1/- and 1/6d in the balcony evenings. When the war broke out it was difficult to light up the place. There was a tiny light in the box office and I had to count out change for the public, but I managed somehow.

On Saturday evening we had two performances and the queue for the second house reached round the corner of Alexander Road from the doors of the Empire. When I had finished I had to check the cash and bag it up. Then I had to carry it in my bag round to the Majestic and hand it over the manager, Percy McCann. After he had checked it I was ready to go home.

Towards the end of my time there I had a scare. As I set off, a man began to follow me, I quickened my steps, so did he, I was nearly at a running pace but my legs were like jelly. In front of me was a man, he looked big and strong and was going my way. I plucked up courage, grabbed his left arm and said, "I need your help, a man is following me and I have money in this bag from the cinema. I'm frightened that he could be after this money. Help me to get to the Majestic, please." He was quite shaken but assured me I would be all right, he took me over the road to the doors of the Majestic then quietly slipped away into the darkness. I told the manager that in future he would have to collect the money. I was not prepared to fight anyone. If they demanded the money, I would hand it over. The manager was not happy about it but arranged for one of his men to collect it in the future.

 An escape from the everyday
Or the place where you earned your pay?

I was a projectionist until about late 1953 or '54, but I had to leave. I'd got no choice. It was through ill health. You see, the old projector used to work with two carbons, one positive and one negative, and when they touched they produced a bright light, which gave you the power to see the film, but it gave off fumes, and it was the fumes that got me, and through that I got pneumonia.

When I recovered, Doctor Fraser, a Newhall doctor, sadly no longer with us, had me in, and he says, "You must get an outside job." I says, "Really!" and he says, "Yes, you must get in the fresh air," and with that I went and got a job with Tunnicliffe the bakers, in Newhall, and I've been a baker ever since. Folks always know when I'm on my way, because I do a bit of yodelling as I walk down the path. I used to do pop grouping and toured abroad - and did summer seasons.

At first we were called *The Phensic Four*. The name was given to us by the landlord at the Wheel Inn, Midway, Fred Rogers, because he said we gave all his customers headaches. One night he came to us and said, "I've got your first booking lads." "Ooh great!" we said, and he replied, "There's a house at Bretby wants haunting!"

Anyway, we became *The Sundowners* in 1962 and we included a girl singer, Denise

Orme. She was 11 years - old when she joined us, and her first song was *My Boy Lollipop*. Later we were known as *The Midways* and people still remember us.

On a Saturday afternoon Brookes buses ran every half hour, and we used to go down to the Majestic, on what would be called now, I suppose, Junior Film Time. Me and my friend would jump off the bus and would run down New Street, which came out at the Old Victoria Inn, at the top of Alexander Hill, and we'd run down the hill, and because the bus had to go a bit of the way round, we would be half way down Alexandra Hill when the bus caught us, and you would see the queue of children coming up the hill, and we would join them.

You could sit anywhere downstairs for tuppence, and you could go upstairs and it was threepence. We went upstairs for threepence, because you could sit at the front there on the balcony and overlook your cronies who were down below. Three elastic bands, looped together and orange peel made a good flirter.

For many the cinema was the only form of relief from work and sleep. Apart from the pub and home there were few places to go except the cinema and of course many of the miners would be on permanent nights so if they wanted to see a film, the only time they could go would be in the morning. That's how miners' matinees came into being. These were of course open to the general public and it cost about half the usual fare to get in. It was a regular thing during term time for the schools' attendance officer to go into the miners' matinees and when the lights came up, see how many kids were sitting in there rather than at their desks!

We adopted the Tommy Dorsey version of 'The Sunny Side' as a signature tune for the cinema - without the vocals - and that would be played at the start and end of each performance, after the National Anthem. When that came on, everyone would stand up. If you happened to be moving when it came on, you'd have to stop dead in your tracks out of respect. All the youngsters, that weren't particularly patriotic would say, "Quick, let's get out before the Queen!" and there'd be a mad rush to get out before it came on!

Grab your coat, grab your hat
Leave your worries on the doorstep
Just direct your feet to the sunny side of the street

One of the conservatives were on the Delph in Swadlincote and he was giving his election address and he says, "You see, if the socialists get in, we shall lose the empire!" and one little lad at the front says, "Ah, but we'll still have the Majestic!"

Back where we started. The clock ticks away
The minutes and hours, no time to stay
On a market place seat and reminisce,
Even though it links the past with this
Day and age. What else remains?
The Market Hall, an inscription, some names
The Delph, The High Street, The Rink Way
Monuments to yesterday
Place names, buildings, streets people trod
But there's something more that makes Swadlincote Swad.